MONROE

# The Monroe Building
## A CHICAGO MASTERPIECE REDISCOVERED

Richard Cahan
and Michael Williams

Photographs by Alexander Vertikoff

Published by CityFiles Press

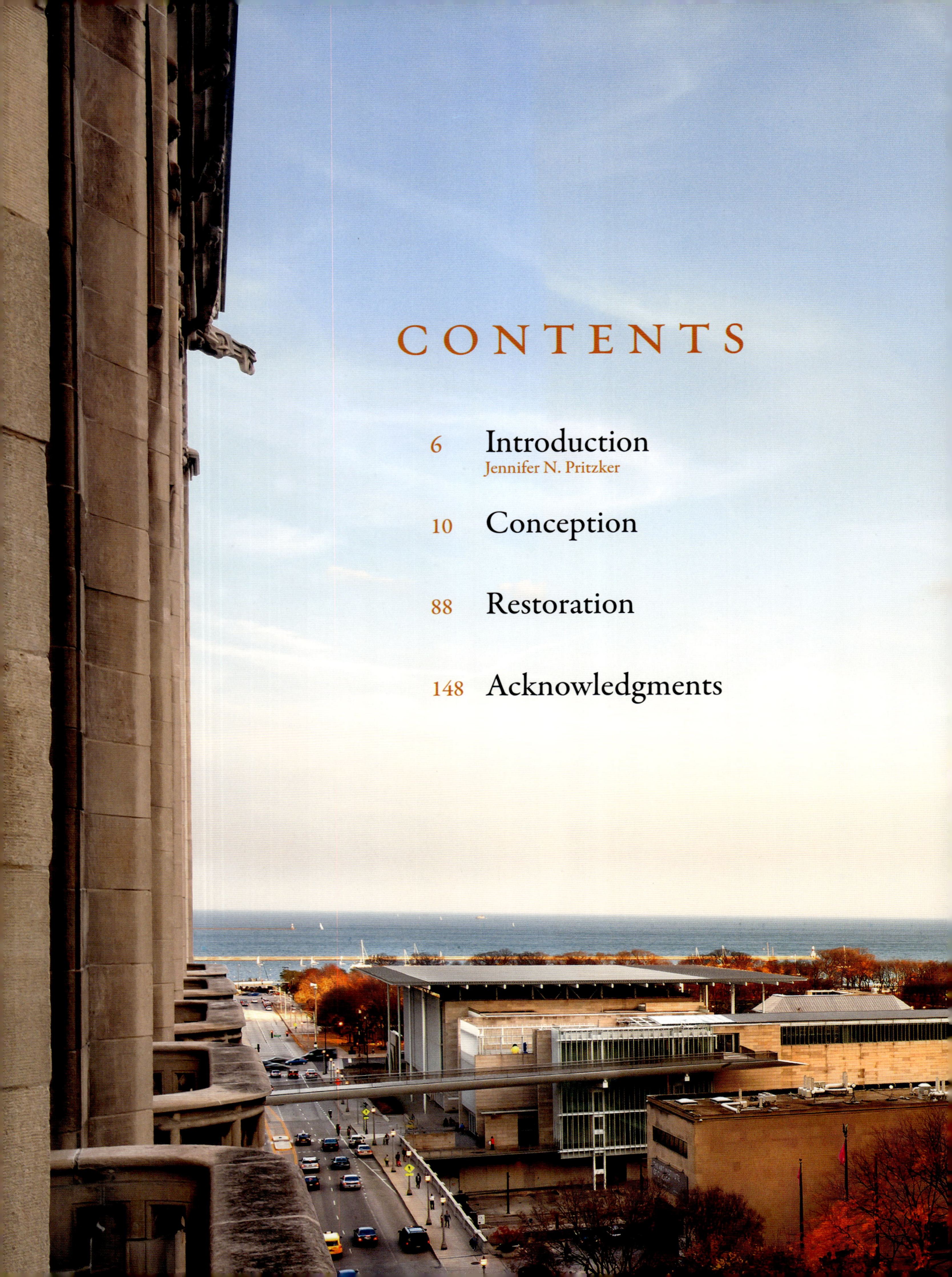

# CONTENTS

# INTRODUCTION

I purchased the Monroe Building as a long-term investment. I wanted to invest in a vintage building and was seeking a suitable home for the Pritzker Military Library. I've done my best to bring back the beauty and grandeur of the early twentieth century, when the building was at the leading edge of commercial architecture. My goal has been to make the Monroe Building functionally relevant for the twenty-first century so that corporations will want to do business here. I want this building to enhance the quality of life and prosperity of all its tenants and users.

History has a way of helping preserve collective and individual identity. It provides a context for what came before us and shows why the world we live in is the way it is. I have always had a deep interest in history. I majored in it in college and worked as a historian in the army during part of my years in the service. All professions rely on case histories to solve problems. Historic preservation of buildings links the study of history to functional and profitable investments.

I follow in the footsteps of my father, the late Robert A. Pritzker, who held a degree in industrial engineering from the Illinois Institute of Technology and a passion for all manner of applied sciences. Architecture was one of them. He helped design our house in Oberlin, Ohio, back in 1953, when he was only twenty-seven. His last years were spent trying to preserve the family summer home in Eagle River, Wisconsin.

About a block away from our Oberlin house was a Frank Lloyd Wright home. Built in the late 1940s, the Weltzheimer House is now owned by Oberlin College, which converted it into an art museum. My family knew the Weltzheimer family, and the house they built was my earliest impression of vintage architecture. Some might classify Wright's Usonian-style home as strictly modern, but like almost all of Wright's work, which I admire, it defies time and classification.

Since those years, I have been moved by other architectural works. Some are world classics, such as the Acropolis in Athens, the Colosseum in Rome, and the Kremlin in Moscow. Some are American classics, such as the Pentagon, the Washington Monument, and New York's Flatiron and Empire State Buildings. And some are Chicago classics, such as the Museum of Science and Industry and the Monadnock Building. All of them elevate me—and reinforce my determination to save exemplary buildings.

Restoration and property management require a serious commitment. Providing a place for people to earn a livelihood or to live is a responsibility. I take pride in offering a safe, healthy space that is also aesthetically pleasing and in delivering a quality product and service that meets the needs and desires of tenants.

Our work on the Monroe Building has not been without challenge. The process of bringing this building back to life has been difficult and expensive. Obtaining the required permits and procedures required has been demanding. But the experience has been worth it; we keep finding hidden surprises beneath just about every layer we encounter. My office on the fifth floor is the best I've ever had.

With the Monroe Building, I am working to contribute to the economic and cultural development of Chicago. Buildings have a life span and need periodic repair and maintenance. A structure as old as the Monroe reaches a point where it must be rebuilt or torn down. We chose a comprehensive restoration—bringing new life to an old building. We took a twentieth-century construction of a nineteenth-century concept (the Chicago skyscraper) and made it relevant and fiscally responsible for the twenty-first century. The Monroe Building, despite its age, was in good enough condition to be fully restored. This restoration enables Chicago to maintain a significant piece of its collective identity.

The building is a functioning monument to the creative energy and spirit that allowed a log cabin settlement to become one of the world's great cities in less than a century. If Chicago wants to remain a world-class city with a vibrant economy, innovative technology, and stimulating intellectual and cultural achievements, it must continue to seek new solutions to old problems.

I hope to continue my own occupation and ownership of the building for as long as it is a positive experience for myself, the people in my organization, the tenants, and the city. I realize that a building must be self-supporting. It must have a positive cash flow and provide a return on investment. I expect the Monroe Building will function at an efficient level, provided it is properly managed and maintained, as it is now. I expect to show profit and a respectable return on investment on a long-term basis.

Not all buildings could be restored like this. Only a handful of organizations or individuals have the capacity to take on such a project. Our team at Tawani Enterprises, with access to capital and an intense interest in history, has made the restoration of the Monroe Building possible. I follow in the tradition of my family by investing in commerce and philanthropy in the place where we live. We hope our work creates a large dividend for all.

Jennifer N. Pritzker
Lieutenant Colonel, U.S. Army (Retired)
President and CEO, Tawani Enterprises

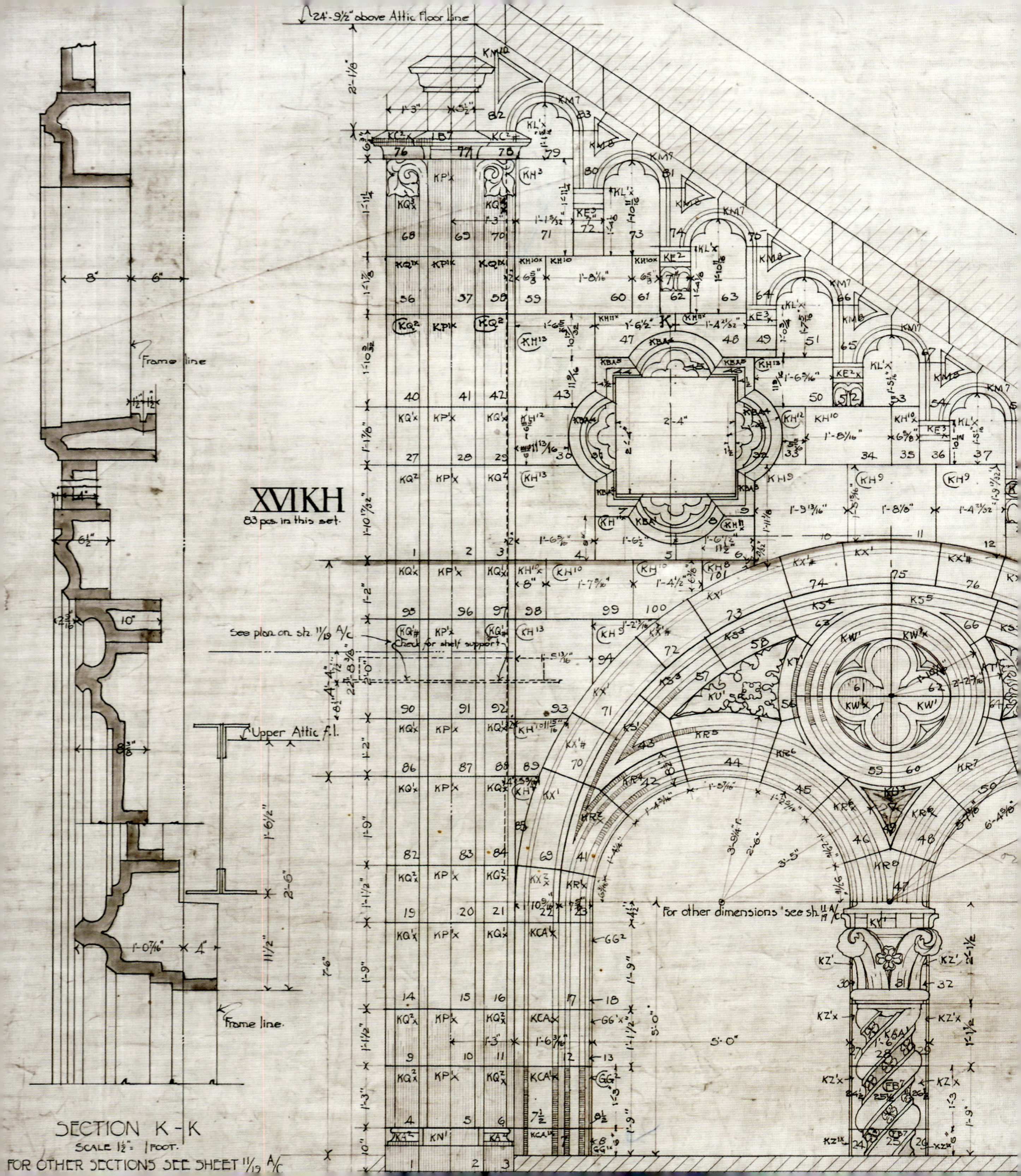

24'-9½" above Attic Floor Line
XVI KH
83 pcs. in this set.
Frame line
Upper Attic f.l.
See plan on sh. 11/19 A/C
Check for shelf support
For other dimensions see sh. 11/19 A/C
Frame line
SECTION K-K
SCALE 1½" = 1 FOOT.
FOR OTHER SECTIONS SEE SHEET 11/19 A/C

# Conception

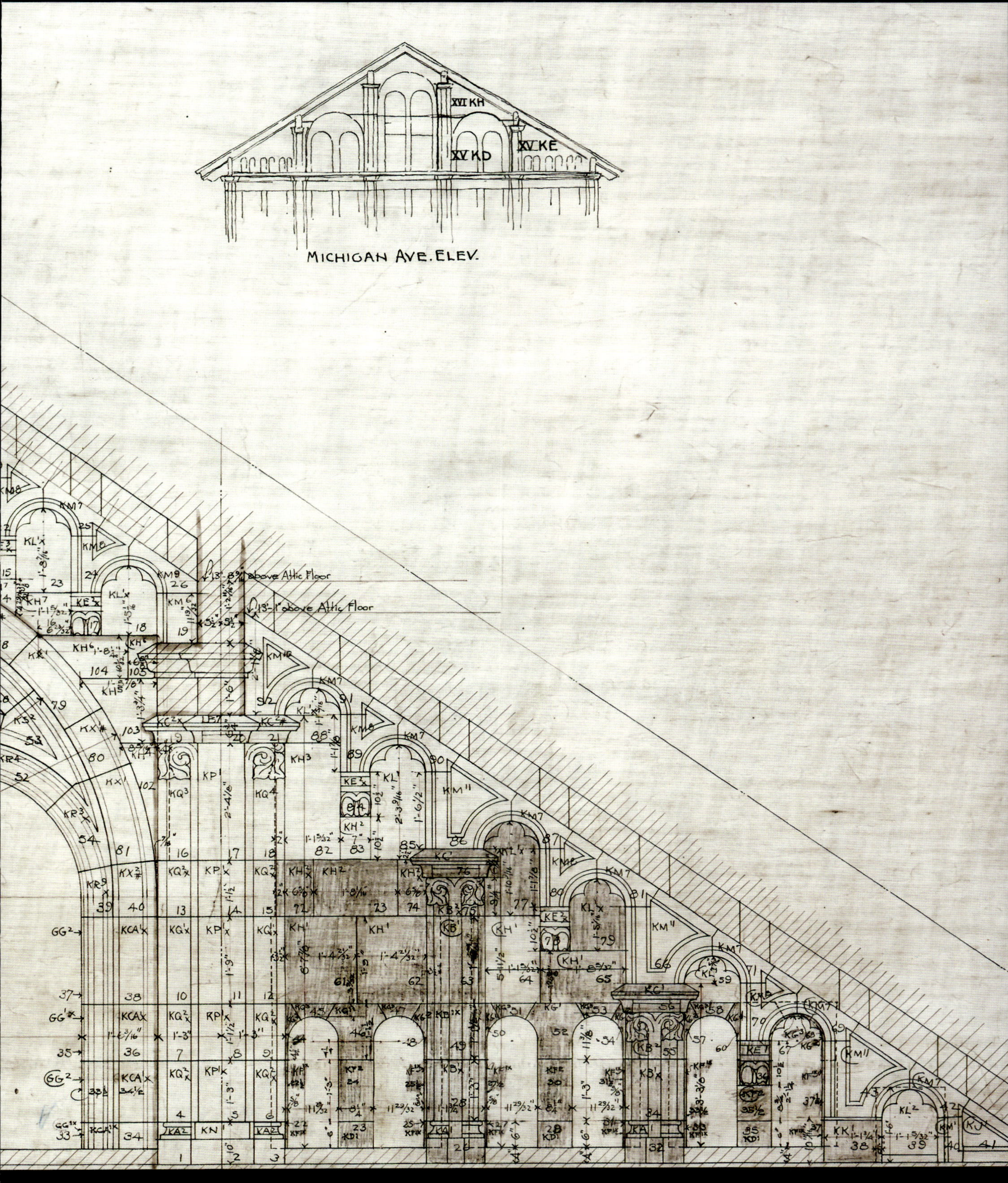


"The genius of Holabird & Roche was showing how to take what was mostly an uninflected box and tweak it just enough to produce something quite distinctive."

Author and historian Robert Bruegmann

**THE MONROE BUILDING IS WHERE THE SKYSCRAPER CAME OF AGE.**

It was built in 1912 by the same team behind some of the world's first tall office buildings. Developers Peter and Shepherd Brooks, architects William Holabird and Martin Roche, and building manager Owen Aldis were at the apex of their careers when they conceived and constructed the sixteen-story building on the eastern edge of the Loop, Chicago's downtown business district.

In the 1880s, they had pioneered the no-nonsense steel-frame office towers that now define modern cities. They discovered how to anchor sturdy foundations into Chicago's gumbo soil, designed wide windows to coax natural light inside, and introduced high-speed elevators that could reach great heights with the casualness of a stroll down a familiar street.

Theirs was a new kind of architecture: soaring buildings with slender grid-like exteriors that masked the skeletons of supporting metal just beneath the surface. Called skyscrapers, their creations evolved, and their style became known as the Chicago School of Architecture.

By 1912, these five men had mastered the skyscraper—how to design it, where to construct it, and how to manage it. "If you track the story, this is where they figured it all out," said Tim Samuelson, Chicago's cultural historian. "They were confident in what they were doing. This is where they pulled it all together."

But here, at 104 South Michigan Avenue, they turned the tables.

**BY THE BEGINNING OF THE TWENTIETH CENTURY,** critics and city dwellers alike found the early skyscrapers of the Chicago School to be harsh and utilitarian—commercial boxes designed for efficiency and not much else. At first glance, the Monroe Building was very much a classic of the Chicago School, with its defined two-story base, big and brawny skeleton, traditional terra-cotta refinements, and tall grid of windows reaching for the sky. But the Monroe rebelled. Its two-story attic roof made clear that this skyscraper was different from most office high-rises of the time.

There is little documentation to indicate that anything extraordinary had been planned for the Monroe, the last building the five men collaborated on. Unlike the work of Louis Sullivan and his disciples, architects who were known for developing an original American style, the Monroe drew on Gothic and Renaissance architectural details for its rounded attic windows, curvy vertical piers, quatrefoil ornamentation, and double barrel vaulted ceilings. A pottery company created tiles for the lobby, and a roofing company produced Spanish tiles (perhaps more suited for a church or university building) for the roof.

Here was a building in the true Arts and Crafts spirit, a terra-cotta fantasy as beautiful as it was functional, a direct challenge to the machine age and the ethos of the Chicago School.

That is what made the building at the southwest corner of Michigan Avenue and Monroe Street, across from Grant Park, so unusual. It was a forerunner of Chicago buildings like the Wrigley Building (begun in 1920 and based on the Giralda Tower of the Seville Cathedral) and Tribune Tower (the neo-Gothic design that won the *Chicago Tribune's* 1922 architecture competition)—downtown office towers that are more about aesthetics than utility.

"I think that by the time of the Monroe Building, there was a strong yearning for a more picturesque and ornamental cityscape," said Robert Bruegmann, who has written extensively on the architectural firm of Holabird & Roche. "Some of the attempts involved very expensive deviations from the standard box. They could be justified because they were corporate buildings and functioned as advertising. The genius of Holabird & Roche as commercial architects was showing how to take what was mostly an uninflected box and tweak it just enough to produce something quite distinctive, ornamental, and exotic."

**WHEN THE MONROE BUILDING OPENED,** Montgomery Schuyler, the most progressive architecture critic of the age, hailed its "unorthodox design." A few years later, owners of the Monroe Building bragged in the *Chicago Central Business and Office Building Directory*: "There is not a more beautiful building in Chicago than the Monroe Building."

Contemporary architects embraced it. Walter Burley Griffin had just installed himself in the new building when he received a telegram informing him that he'd won a prestigious international design competition. His rival Frank Lloyd Wright moved in briefly a few years later, maintaining his Chicago office in the sixteenth-floor loft.

But the building was seldom more than a footnote in the architectural history of the city, forgotten by the critics who invented the idea of the Chicago School. These modernists saw the Chicago skyscrapers of the 1880s and 1890s as precursors to the stripped-down steel-and-glass structures of the post–World War II era, so they had no interest in the Monroe, with its broad gable roof and side dormers that were as familiar and welcoming as an American bungalow.

Historians of the Chicago School, including Lewis Mumford in the 1920s, Sigfried Giedion in the 1940s, and Carl Condit in the 1950s and 1960s, rarely mentioned it, partly because it wasn't exceedingly tall or exceptionally massive or particularly innovative, but mostly because it sported architectural details that looked back rather than forward.

"It is exactly these qualities that disqualified it from the modernist canon but that make it so attractive to us today," said Bruegmann. For almost a century, the Monroe Building was largely ignored. It stood forgotten, covered in downtown soot and grime.

**EDWARD A. RENWICK, A PARTNER AT THE FIRM HOLABIRD & ROCHE,** remembered when Peter Brooks first proposed that the Monroe Building should complement the neighboring University Club of Chicago: "He took us across into Grant Park and looking back at the University Club, [and] said, 'Mr. Roche and Mr. Renwick, I consider the University Club a beautiful building. You build a building on my lot which shall be harmonious with it. The height and the character shall be left to you.'"

Renwick was a keen observer of Chicago's architectural life, and his 1932 *Recollections* helps scholars better understand the period and the firm. But his account of this incident is curious for several reasons. It was Shepherd Brooks, not Peter Brooks, who took the lead on the Monroe. The brothers, who lived in Boston, rarely came to Chicago. And the earliest Holabird & Roche rendering of the Monroe shows a neo-Gothic building with a hip roof rather than the gable roof that imitates the University Club's.

OWEN F. ALDIS

Regardless, by the time the first official drawing of the Monroe was shown to the public in the November 19, 1910, issue of *The Economist,* the original rendering had changed dramatically. Its fifteen-story building had morphed into a fourteen-story one with a two-story attic beneath the distinctive gable roof. The accompanying article indicated that plans for the building were already well under way:

> Aldis & Company announce that the Brooks estate has definitely decided to begin on the first of May next the erection of a handsome building at the southwest corner of Michigan Avenue and Monroe Street. It will be known as the Monroe building. Plans have been drawn by Holabird & Roche and accepted. These plans show a building fourteen stories and an attic high, with a gabled roof. It will thus balance nicely with the University Club on the opposite corner. The exterior of the lower two floors will be of polished granite and the upper floors of gray terra cotta. The design is somewhat Gothic in style and it is hoped that the building will be harmonious in every way with its surroundings and particularly with the University Club on the opposite corner and the Illinois Athletic Club adjoining it on the north. There will be one handsome entrance in the center of the Michigan avenue frontage and another entrance on Monroe street, both leading to the central hallway and the seven passenger elevators. The building will be completed on May 1, 1912. Each floor will contain about 11,000 square feet of very well lighted rentable space, and Messrs. Aldis & Company, the agents, propose to rent it generally to tenants requiring rather large amounts of space.

The following day, the *Chicago Tribune* detailed plans about the Monroe and another building at Monroe and Clark Streets, four blocks to the west. "Both of the proposed buildings should add greatly to the prestige of this rapidly coming street," it noted, "while the Monroe building, as the structure at the corner of Michigan avenue is called, means not only another handsome structure for the avenue, but also another artistic addition to that exceedingly handsome group of buildings represented by the University Club building and

MICHIGAN AVENUE AT MONROE STREET IN 1908. THE UNIVERSITY CLUB OF CHICAGO HAS JUST BEEN CONSTRUCTED. THE GLASSY, TWO-STORY BUILDING ACROSS THE STREET, DESIGNED FOR THE BROOKS BROTHERS BY HOLABIRD & ROCHE, IS ON THE SITE OF THE MONROE BUILDING. (CHICAGO HISTORY MUSEUM PHOTO)

AN EARLY SKETCH OF MONROE BUILDING SHOWS A FIFTEEN-STORY BUILDING WITH A STANDARD HIP ROOF.

that of the Illinois Athletic Club, just to the south of the new Monroe."

The *Tribune* reported that construction of the Monroe Building would not exceed $1 million. (Decades later the cost was put at $1.2 million.) The men's clothing store Capper & Capper would occupy a corner on its first floor, and the shoe store French, Shriner & Urner would take up the rest of the Monroe Street frontage. The Mahin Advertising Company would lease the tenth floor, and Holabird & Roche signed up for the fourteenth floor. Other announced tenants included the Great Lakes Dredge & Dock Company, the Strauss Bascule Bridge Company, and the Tea Shop, which had been in the building demolished to make way for the Monroe. Photographer William Koehne would set up his studio in the large, well-lit attic space.

"The closing of so many leases so long in advance of the completion of the building is a striking indication of the ripeness of the situation," the *Tribune* observed.

In March 1911, the paper's art and architecture critic, Harriet Monroe, wrote that architectural drawings of the Monroe Building were shown at the annual exhibition of the Chicago Architecture Club at the Art Institute. She called the Monroe "an interesting Gothic design" and described the building as a "sixteen story gable roofed edifice of admirable proportions which is to stand opposite the University Club, by the same architects, and agreeably complement its design." But Harriet Monroe, who later founded and edited *Poetry* magazine, was not as impressed with the plans as she was with Cass Gilbert's drawings for the fifty-seven-story Woolworth Building in New York City. "To have made a thing of beauty out of such a huge commercial colossus is a triumph of inventive genius," she declared.

It wasn't until April 1912, a month before the Monroe Building opened, that a critique of it appeared in a national publication. The influential architecture critic and journalist Montgomery Schuyler, writing under the pseudonym Franz Winkler in *The Architectural Record,* said that the Monroe was a business building with just enough ornament that expressed its structure. What caught his eye was the gable roof, the Monroe's most distinctive feature, which he questioned from a financial standpoint but admired from an artistic one. "Whether, simply as the administrator of an investment, the architect is justified in a gable roof instead of continuing his walls to the usual uncouth parallelepiped may be questionable, but at any rate the sensitive spectator will thank him for having found the variation permissible."

**CHICAGO IS REGARDED AS THE BIRTHPLACE OF THE SKYSCRAPER** by most everyone outside of New York City. After the fire of 1871 swept away the remains of the prairie city, Chicago's vacant downtown was available and primed for development. But the choice building area was small, hemmed in by the Chicago River on the north and the west, Lake Michigan on the east, and a mass of railroad tracks to the south. By the 1880s, it was clear that the central business district had to grow vertically if it was to expand.

The upward trajectory of new buildings was remarkably steady.

William Le Baron Jenney's Portland Block was erected the year after the fire, followed by John Van Osdel's eight-story Chicago Real Estate Exchange in 1873. Daniel Burnham and John Wellborn Root's ten-story Montauk Building, considered by some to be the first skyscraper, was built in 1882, topped two years later by Jenney's ten-story Home Insurance Building, at the time one of the tallest office towers in the world. Next up was W. W. Boyington's thirteen-story Royal Insurance Building in 1885, which was dwarfed by Dankmar Adler and Louis Sullivan's eighteen-story Auditorium Building in 1889. In 1892, Burnham and Root raised the roof again with their twenty-one-story Masonic Temple, which was not bested until 1909, when the Blackstone and the La Salle Hotels, both twenty-two stories, were built.

But the ascension was slowed by politics. Tall buildings frightened people. As early as 1891 (less than three years after the term "sky-scraper" first appeared), the *Chicago Tribune* wrote about the possibility of putting restrictions on height. The newspaper interviewed architects, "real-estate men," and doctors who shared concerns about the safety and impact of skyscrapers. High-rises tended to centralize commerce downtown, they said, and destroy businesses in outlying neighborhoods. The towering structures hogged light and air, creating unhealthy "sanitary conditions."

Even Jenney, the father of the American skyscraper, was quoted in the *Tribune* as saying: "Architects are not in favor of sky-scraping structures as is popularly supposed. We advise our clients to limit their buildings to twelve stories on the ground of economy as well as general safety." Exceeding tall buildings, he said, are not practical because elevators take up space throughout the building and the thick lower walls needed to support the buildings take up lower floor space. "The present high buildings of Chicago are the best and most substantial in the world," Jenney continued. "They represent the honor of capable architects and honest builders. The danger in high buildings comes from unscrupulous architects."

Chicago responded to these concerns by limiting the height of skyscrapers. In 1893, the city council prohibited new buildings over 130 feet, or ten stories. That was raised to 155 feet in 1896, lowered back to 130 feet in 1898, and raised to 180 feet in 1901 and to 260 feet in 1902. But in 1910, the year the Monroe Building was designed, the height limit was lowered once again, this time to 200 feet, or sixteen stories.

According to Edward Renwick, his firm ingeniously circumvented the council's 1893 height limit. Holabird & Roche received news on a Thursday afternoon of the upcoming Monday vote. It pulled permits and hired forty draftsmen (it normally had eight) to work twelve-hour shifts over those four days to draw up plans for five buildings: the south end of the Monadnock, the Marquette Building, the Old Colony Building, the Champlain Building, and a building at Madison and Michigan. All but the last were constructed.

**IT MAY BE HARD TO BELIEVE**, but Michigan Avenue—now the most prime real estate in Chicago—was something of a rural backwater throughout most of

the nineteenth century. Asked a reader in the *Tribune:* "Do you remember 'way back when' in the early '80s, Cooper's mule pens were located on the present site of Monroe Building, Michigan and Monroe, and there you could see your Missouri friends peeping through the knotholes in the high board fence, kept immaculate in whitewash?"

In 1872, Walter S. Gurnee, a tanner who briefly served as the mayor of Chicago, built an elegant brick mansion on the southwest corner of Michigan and Monroe. In 1885, the property—Lot 1 and a tiny sliver of Lot 4 in Block 4 of Fractional Section 15—was purchased by Shepherd Brooks and his wife, Clara, for $186,000. (Though Shepherd and Clara Brooks are listed as the owners of the property in the Cook County recorder of deeds office, contemporary accounts included Peter Brooks in all transactions regarding the site.)

A high-pitched two-story structure housing a tailor shop was built on the site in 1888. Known as a taxpayer, the building brought in enough

THE CITY BEFORE THE SKYSCRAPER BOOM. LOOKING NORTH ON LASALLE STREET AT RANDOLPH STREET IN 1894. HIGH-SPEED ELEVATORS, ELECTRIC LIGHTING AND ADVANCES IN CONSTRUCTION MADE SKYSCRAPERS POSSIBLE.

MICHIGAN AVENUE WAS A ONE-SIDED STREET SINCE 1836, WHEN LAKE PARK (LATER GRANT PARK) WAS CREATED. LOOKING SOUTH ON MICHIGAN AVENUE AT JACKSON STREET IN 1887, ABOUT TWO BLOCKS SOUTH OF THE MONROE BUILDING SITE. EARLY MANSIONS ON THE STREET GAVE WAY TO HOTELS, OFFICE BUILDINGS AND BUILDINGS WITH LIGHT MANUFACTURING.

HOTEL

rent money to cover the taxes and allowed the Brookses to perch on the site, waiting for a speculative project. In 1892, a natural gas explosion rocked several blocks of Monroe Street and blew out all twenty-four of the building's plate-glass windows. Around the turn of the century, the tailor shop was joined by a tea shop that catered to high society. By 1911, the glass-fronted building that would be torn down for the Monroe Building was home to a mix of businesses, including a lunchroom, a cigar shop, stores that sold Irish and Japanese goods, and the Peerless Lighting Company.

SHEPHERD BROOKS

It was during the first two decades of the 1900s that Michigan Avenue became the upscale eastern border of the downtown business district. Right across from the new lakefront park named for President Ulysses S. Grant in 1901, the street was widened and illuminated by fancy streetlamps. Skyscrapers followed. The seventeen-story Railway Exchange Building (later known as the Santa Fe Building) opened on it in 1904, and the fifteen-story Harvester Building (now part of Columbia College) was built in 1907. The ten-story Illinois Athletic Club (adjacent to the Monroe Building on the south) and the twelve-story University Club (just to the north) opened in 1908. The twenty-one-story People's Gas Building opened in 1910. The Monroe Building opened two years later.

**THE BROOKS BROTHERS WERE AMONG THE MOST PROMINENT DEVELOPERS** in Chicago despite the fact that they were based in Massachusetts. They purchased a huge amount of property in Chicago's downtown because they didn't think they could lose. "Tall buildings will pay well in Chicago hereafter, and sooner or later a way will be found to erect them," wrote Peter Brooks in 1881. He was right.

The brothers were heirs of Peter Chardon Brooks I. The New England merchant made a fortune as a marine insurance broker and was one of the richest men in America. His Harvard-educated grandsons Peter Chardon Brooks III and Shepherd Brooks saw a great opportunity in investing their own money and the money of fellow New Englanders in America's boomtown following the Great Chicago Fire.

Peter, born in 1831, was the practical brother, an ornery moneyman who didn't waste a cent. Shepherd, born six years later, was more of an idealist. He had studied architecture and then traveled throughout Europe before returning to Massachusetts, where he lived the life of a country gentleman, spending decades creating an expansive estate just north of Boston. "He had a house in Boston and a beautiful estate in the western part of Medford, where he indulged his tastes for rural life and raised extensive crops of the highest quality," noted the Medford Historical Society. "The Brooks estate was one of the show places of Medford, and was famed throughout the East." Shepherd and Peter, who described themselves as "practical farmers," built summer homes there.

The brothers did all of their Chicago investing through Owen F. Aldis, a lawyer and the perfect link to the metropolis of the Midwest. The son of a prominent Vermont judge named Asa Owen Aldis, he moved to Chicago in 1875 to become the point man for New Englanders interested in investing in the rebounding city. Peter Brooks hired him in 1879 to manage one of the brothers' first buildings, the Portland Block, in the heart of the downtown district.

Aldis was tall and heavy and, according to Edward Renwick, had a kindly face and a brilliant mind. "He was one of the most broad minded real estate operators I have ever known," Renwick wrote. "He had a great advantage in being the sole agent for one of the wealthiest estates in Boston, the Brooks estate, which gave him control of some eastern capital. It was a great thing in those days to have control of eastern capital, for Chicago had so little capital of its own. It had plenty of energy and plenty of energetic men like Phil Armour and the McCormicks, but they were busy building up their own businesses which required every bit of capital they could muster."

PETER BROOKS

Aldis corresponded with Peter and Shepherd Brooks for decades through thousand of letters and telegrams. The relationship bloomed from the start. Wrote Shepherd early on: "I need not say that you have been a very satisfactory agent and that we should . . . hope that the same favorable relationship may continue as long as possible."

The brothers' early purchases were usually on the fringe of downtown Chicago, specifically west of Wabash Avenue between Van Buren and Taylor Streets. Writing about the area where the Monadnock Building was built, Renwick stated: "There was nothing on the south side of the street between State street and the river but cheap, one-story shacks, mere hovels. Everyone thought Mr. Aldis was insane to build way out here on the ragged edge of the city. Later when he carried the building on through to Van Buren Street they were sure he was." But it was one of the best investments the Brooks' brothers made.

The purchases were driven by Aldis, who wrote: "I prefer real estate for investment and know of no better place than Chicago for it." In hindsight, it seems obvious. Aldis studied Chicago's downtown and determined that business and activity must move south of Van Buren: "The retail business of the original town must expand chiefly in that direction."

In 1887, Aldis—using a swan quill pen from London—wrote the Brookses:

> I am inclined to think that if nothing happens to impede the growth of Chicago within ten years every lot will be solidly and substantially built up and filled up in the center of the City. Of course some buildings will by that time be torn down and rebuilt, and all under ninety feet high will be raised to six stories or ninety feet. This means, of course, an immense compressing of business population in the Center. Then rents must rise largely, many kinds of business will be forced out of the Center, many others must pay enormously high rents, or contract the space occupied by them. When that time comes it does not seem to me improbable that such corners as Dearborn and Monroe will be worth from $60 to $100 per square foot, and that a fair ground rental would be three times what you now get. This time may be five or it may be fifteen years, but it must come.

HOLABIRD & ROCHE DESIGNED THE SOUTH HALF OF THE MONADNOCK BUILDING, WHICH EXTENDED THE BUILDING ON DEARBORN STREET TO VAN BUREN STREET IN 1893. COSTS WERE MUCH CHEAPER THAN THE NORTH HALF, WHICH WAS DESIGNED BY BURNHAM & ROOT TWO YEARS EARLIER.

Aldis and the Brookses posted an early string of successes that made them the premier developers of Chicago and helped them redefine the city's downtown. In 1881, they gave Burnham and Root their first major commission, the seven-story Grannis Block on Dearborn Street. "Here our originality began to show," wrote Burnham. "We made the front of the building all red, the terra-cotta exactly matching the brick. It was a wonder. Everybody went to see it, and the town was proud of it."

The world took notice of the next collaboration between the Brookses and Burnham and Root. In 1882, they produced the ten-story Montauk Building, one of the world's first skyscrapers. "What Chartres was to the Gothic cathedral, the Montauk Block was to the high commercial building," wrote architect and critic Thomas Tallmadge.

Although Aldis considered Root a genius—"No other man ever impressed me so quickly and so deeply," he said—he did not hesitate to relay architectural cues from Peter Brooks, the bottom-line guy determined to make his buildings pay. "The building throughout is to be for use and not for ornament," Brooks wrote Aldis in 1881. "Its beauty will be in its all-adaption to its use." Brooks stressed that buildings must be solid enough to look strong and handsome enough to attract interest. But he stressed being practical. Projections on the front facade were discouraged because they would catch dirt; picture moldings were to be placed near the ceiling so that hooks did not deface walls. "The less plumbing the less trouble," he wrote. "Colored glass is mere nonsense, a passing fashion, inappropriate in a mercantile building and worse than all, it obstructs the light. Strike it all out."

Brooks, the client, guided Burnham and Root. "Peter Brooks is the one who made them shape up," said historian Tim Samuelson. "He helped create the Chicago aesthetic."

Burnham & Root's next project for the Brookses was the eleven-story Rookery, one of Chicago's foremost landmarks, on LaSalle Street in the heart of the city's financial district. Completed in 1888, it was caught in the transition between two ages of commercial construction. Structurally, it is held up by a combination of load-bearing exterior walls and a metal cage supporting the interior. Aesthetically, The Rookery was not as stripped down as the Montauk, perhaps because The Rookery was home to high-rolling commodity traders, lawyers, and bankers. Here the developers and architects found a reason to add granite, brick, and terra-cotta ornament of many styles. And here they topped the building with six pinnacles. "I'm still ambivalent about the use of ornament," wrote Root during the construction, "because decoration should never be applied to conceal the outline and intent of the more elementary and essential features of the building."

One year later, Holabird & Roche took the metal-cage idea and broke the box. The twelve-story Tacoma Building was the first structure to use an interior metal grid for support. Wrought-iron beams and cast-iron columns held the weight of the building; its exterior masonry walls simply served as skin. Projecting over the sidewalks on LaSalle and Madison Streets, those thin walls with their large windows gave the impression that the building was tipsy. "Many people have an idea that it is a mere shell set up on pins, and that if two wide-awake blizzards should ever happen to meet in Chicago it would come down with a great flop from its high perch," the *Tribune* reported.

The Tacoma was the first tall building designed by Holabird & Roche, the firm that would draw the plans for the Monroe Building. The lead builder of the Monroe, Paul Starrett, who went on to supervise the construction of the Flatiron and Empire State Buildings in New York City, declared that the gutsy Tacoma was the first skyscraper. "The steel framework on the street fronts supported the *entire structure, outer walls and all,"* he wrote. "As I look back, I can't remember that the Tacoma Building excited any special comment. It was merely the logical conclusion toward which the wide-awake architects of Chicago had been moving, pushed by necessity and led by opportunity."

Just as the Brooks brothers helped direct architects like Burnham and Root and Holabird and Roche, Owen Aldis helped direct the Brookses. He is the one who worked out a successful business formula for constructing and maintaining a tall building on a small piece of land. He totaled the costs of operating buildings and figured out what was needed to make a building attractive, practical, efficient—and profitable. He was the pioneer of making the skyscrapers work.

Wrote historian Donald L. Miller in *City of the Century*:

> William E. Hale's high-speed hydraulic elevators made tall buildings feasible, but it was Aldis who convinced wary investment clients to build them. By the end of the century, he was managing almost 20 percent of Chicago's downtown office space for real estate speculators. He had a commanding influence—amounting almost to a veto—on the layout and design of high office buildings, a greater influence, in many instances, than that of the architects.
>
> His power arose naturally from the character of the buildings he supervised. They were speculations, and the business that was conducted in them, it must be remembered, could easily have been conducted elsewhere, as it was, for example, in London or Paris, in three- and four-story "walk-ups." Tall building were built in Chicago because real estate property managers like Aldis were able to convince speculators organized into investment pools that they could bring tall profits. And these risky investments eventually became profitable because these same property managers were able to convince companies, small and large, that the most convenient and efficient way to conduct their affairs was in a building of ten or more stories, where they could share space with firms with whom they did business. The skyscraper, Aldis argued, made it far easier to do business in Chicago than in London, where much time was wasted in going from firm to firm all over the sprawling city and climbing the steep stairs of run-down buildings to small, poorly lit offices that were dusty and foul-smelling.

**BY THE TURN OF THE CENTURY,** Aldis had accumulated a set of rules that guided the Brooks brothers and other clients in their real estate investments.

THE BROOKS BROTHERS' MOST ENDURING SUCCESS WAS THE ROOKERY, DESIGNED BY BURNHAM & ROOT AT 209 LASALLE STREET AND COMPLETED IN 1888.

HOLABIRD & ROCHE'S TACOMA BUILDING, THIRD FROM RIGHT, RISES ABOVE LASALLE STREET AT MADISON STREET, ABOUT 1890. ONE OF THE FIRST SKYSCRAPERS EVER BUILT, IT WAS TORN DOWN IN 1929.

He advised them to pay special attention to the most visible parts of the building: the lobby, elevators cabs, corridors, and bathrooms. And he cautioned them not to underestimate the value of small-office tenants, who did not swamp the elevators or move as a group and, more important, could be charged more.

In 1893, Aldis wrote Peter Brooks his most important rule: "Second-class space costs as much to build and operate as first-class space. Therefore, build no second-class space."

When not investing in buildings, Aldis invested in books, amassing a remarkable collection of first editions by American authors, which he donated to his alma mater, Yale University. At the time, the school called it the most extensive trove of its kind, and it became the basis for the Yale Collection of American Literature. Aldis said he spent decades on the hunt, finding forgotten volumes in dusty bookstalls and corresponding with the literary lights of the day. He gathered letters from James Fenimore Cooper, Nathaniel Hawthorne, Henry Wadsworth Longfellow, Walt Whitman, Edgar Allan Poe, Henry David Thoreau, and Harriet Beecher Stow and did translations. One of his own poems, "To a Mocking Bird," was published in the prestigious *Poetry* magazine.

But by 1911, the year of his Yale donation, the bibliophile was finding this work less satisfying. He lamented that it was getting harder to acquire significant material: "Collecting is not a game now as it used to be. The prize belongs now to the man who has the most money to pay. The men who get the books now are those who sit at home and have commissionaires out on the market to buy in rarities as they might buy in chickens. Only the rich can play at it now."

Literature was an important sideline for Aldis, but his collecting depended on his skill as a real estate developer and property manager. Aldis and the Brooks brothers had come to depend more and more on the firm of Holabird & Roche following John Root's death, at forty-one, in 1891. Like Burnham & Root (later D. H. Burnham & Company), Holabird & Roche could design just about any type of structure. Burnham & Root got off to a faster start in the 1880s, but by the 1900s Holabird & Roche was comparable in size. It was known for designing no-nonsense Chicago-style buildings that stood on a strong grid. The firm worked quickly, without cost overruns, and was noted for its engineering excellence. In 1893, Holabird & Roche was hired by the Brooks brothers to design the south portion of the Monadnock Building. Technology had changed since Burnham & Root designed the north half. Instead of using a load-bearing form of construction, Holabird & Roche worked out an ingenious steel-frame grid system.

This is where his young firm proved itself, Edward Renwick wrote:

> The south end of the Monadnock Block proved to be a great stepping-stone to business for our firm. Owen F. Aldis, the financial agent for a good many buildings representing Boston capital, was agent for this

> block. The north half of the block had been done by Burnham and Root, a 68-by-200 foot building, masonry piers, steel inner columns, steel beams, and regular tile arch fireproof construction. The south end was exactly the same size as to its lot, to be carried up to the same height with the same number of stories. We had the advantage of the study of the north half in designing the south. The south half was a skeleton building, the arrangement of the elevators was materially changed, also the location of staircases. When it was finished Mr. Aldis stated, in our office, that the new building cost 15 percent less than the north, contained 15 to 16 percent more available renting space and that space [was] 15 percent lighter than the space of the north half. "This makes me decide," he said, "that I can no longer afford to employ another architect."

WILLIAM HOLABIRD

Renwick wrote that Holabird & Roche was unique among the star firms of the day in that it didn't tell clients what their buildings should look like. Instead, the firm's partners listened. "We realized clearly that you could learn a lot from the owner, in fact Owen Aldis taught more about the requirements of an office building and the way to satisfy tenants than anyone else," Renwick remarked. "That was, I should say, the chief difference between Holabird & Roche and other architectural firms, that we realized the owner could contribute to the success of the building. That led in the end to satisfied clients."

By 1911, the year that the Monroe Building plans were announced, Holabird & Roche had an imposing portfolio of Chicago commercial buildings, including the Tacoma (1889), Pontiac (1891), Monadnock (1893), Old Colony (1894), Champlain (1894), Marquette (1895), Williams (1898), Chicago (1905), Republic (1905), and Brooks (1907). The firm did not possess the artistic flair of Louis Sullivan or John Root, but it did create the Chicago window. The three-part window consisting of smaller double-hung sash windows flanking a larger central fixed pane became a trademark of the commercial style. It was practical, letting in lots of light, and beautiful.

Architectural historian and critic Carl Condit declared Holabird & Roche the most consistent firm in Chicago. Although it was criticized for the uniformity of its buildings, he wrote, it maintained high standards: "Individual buildings of Sullivan and Root are superior to anything they did, yet they discovered the simplest utilitarian and structural solutions to the problems of the big urban office block, and out of these solutions they developed a perfectly rational and standardized form adaptable with minor variations to the conditions imposed by the commercial structure in a crowded urban area."

**LIKE DANIEL BURNHAM, THE RAINMAKER AT BURNHAM & ROOT,** William Holabird was a substantial presence about town. At six foot three, he gave speeches on hunting grizzly bears and was driven around in a Pierce-Arrow motorcar. "All I remember is this absolutely monster image with a very bristly white beard that hurt when you kissed," recalled his grandson John Holabird

Jr. "He was gruff, with a deep voice. He could scare the daylights out of any of his draftsmen."

But he was well liked, too, and was known by many young men in real estate and architecture as Uncle Bill. In 1902, when Holabird was nominated to serve as president of the Western Golf Association, the *Chicago Tribune* declared that "a more popular selection could hardly have been made."

A military brat, William Holabird was born in 1854 in the tiny town of Amenia Union, New York. His father, Quartermaster General of the Army Samuel Beckley Holabird, was credited with inventing the pup tent. William grew up in St. Paul, Minnesota, and attended the U.S. Military Academy at West Point. He resigned and moved to Chicago in 1875 to work as a draftsman for William Le Baron Jenney, the engineer-turned-architect who conceived the steel-frame skyscraper. Holabird met Martin Roche there, and they started their own firm in 1881.

MARTIN ROCHE

Unlike other prominent architects of the day, Holabird did not claim to be a design genius. "Our buildings are eminently sane," he told the *Tribune* in 1911. "On the exterior as well as the interior there is no over-abundance of ornament, no lavish display of wealth. Space is utilized to a degree of economy not reached in any other city, yet without the building suffering there-from. In their conception, the demands of capital have been paramount, yet with it all this sense of economy, almost bordering on frugality, has not been allowed to so influence builders as to injure the general appearance and beauty of these mammoth structure."

Holabird had a good eye and oversaw projects, but he left most of the design work to Roche and the engineering to engineers. The firm Ritter & Mott engineered the Monroe Building. "In the office Holabird never made any drawings, he was not a designer," recalled Renwick. "He never did much in engineering either. He was an excellent critic, he knew the styles, and he had good taste. He could make remarks which would completely spoil a design for you, for instance, one time Roche had a design made and Holabird looking at it said, 'It looks just like a Saratoga trunk.' From that time on that was all you could see in it."

Holabird had a touch of a superiority complex, Renwick said, and made quick decisions: "He was apt to decide almost instantly whether or not a thing interested him. He was very forceful. He was a great reader, and had the gift which his father and grandfather before him had, of being able to grasp the whole contents of a page at a glance, and also the memory to retain it for years. He could take a book, a complicated work on engineering, home in the evening and bring it back the next morning. Five years later a dispute might come up and Holabird would say, 'Here, give me that book,' and turning almost instantly to the page he would point out the quotation which he had remembered."

Holabird was a family man, with a wife and six children. He also made friends easily and had many connections. A good talker and well informed, he brought in the bulk of the firm's commissions by belonging to clubs and

THE VARIETY OF HOLABIRD & ROCHE'S CHICAGO SKYSCRAPERS: THE 1899 MCCLURG, ONLY EIGHTY FEET WIDE AND NINE STORIES TALL, WAS ONE OF THE SMALLEST CHICAGO SKYSCRAPERS. THE 1895 MARQUETTE WAS MASSIVE AT SIXTEEN STORIES AND 229 FEET TALL.

traveling widely to meet potential clients. His reputation for honesty greatly helped the firm, and so did his business sense. As *The Economist* pointed out following his death in 1923, it was more important to Holabird that a building work financially than aesthetically.

Martin Roche was Holabird's exact opposite. He was shy, a lifelong bachelor who suffered from curvature of the spine. He shared a house on the South Side with his sister and her family and kept a daily diary, filled with little more than notations about his long work hours (including Saturdays and Sundays), obligations, chores, and occasional fishing trips to the North Pond or Wisconsin. On the day he arrived back in Chicago from a 1910 trip to Europe, where he visited the Sistine Chapel, Roche wrote: "Met by Messrs. Holabird, Renwick and Smith and Mrs. Leong and Margaret. Went directly to the office. All office all day. Home all evening." In a 1906 *Tribune* article titled "Architect Is Man of Woes; Carries Burdens of Many," he wrote that an architect's life was filled with "work and worries that bring gray hairs before his time."

Born in Cleveland in 1855, a year after Holabird, Roche came to Chicago as a child. He dropped out of school at twelve to work in a bottle factory. In 1872, he started at Jenney's firm as an office boy, eventually rising to head draftsman. "He studied design, as everyone else did in those days, by working with someone who was experienced," Renwick wrote. "When you consider Roche's lack of opportunity you think that he had genius to get as far as he did."

In 1881, Holabird approached Roche about joining his tiny firm. At the time, Holabird was moonlighting, supplementing his modest earnings as an architect by working nights as an army clerk. He asked Roche how little he could live on. Roche told him forty dollars a month, and he became a partner in the new firm, Holabird & Roche.

Roche, reported Renwick, had a "high and inflexible standard of conduct" that both helped and hindered him: "Roche was a man without guile, trusting almost anyone, but if he once thought the one he had trusted deviated from absolute sincerity he would have nothing more to do with him. That made him at times terribly stubborn."

Roche, the inside guy, was the firm's lead designer. Holabird rounded up clients, and Roche made sure they got what they wanted. "First, it frequently is necessary for the architect to use every endeavor to make the man who has the money realize the full possibilities of the project from an architectural as well as from a business standpoint," Roche wrote. "Not until this is accomplished is the architect prepared to take up the serious side of his real work."

Taking pencil to paper was only a small part of his job. "The public has an odd idea of the scope of work of the architect," Roche noted. "If it were to outfit him, it would give him a set of drawing instruments, cardboard, a drawing board, and a window having a north light. Out of this it would expect him to make name and fortune."

And even then, he said, the work was complex and often dreary. "One building which the architect has designed and which is accepted by the owner may involve 125,000 words of typewritten specifications, copied and bound into as many as thirty editions."

Holabird concurred, writing in 1911 in the *Tribune:*

> The preliminary preparations for a building involving millions is no small matter, especially in view of the fact that every detail must be prepared months in advance. Not the least of these is the financing and other negotiations; then, for months and months before the public sees evidences of a building, a small army of men has been burrowing underground, shoring existing buildings, and sinking mammoth shafts of concrete into the earth 100 feet or more below grade, to solid rock upon which the future building must stand. Sometimes several years elapse between the conception and the culmination of an enterprise. Then again, enterprises lie dormant for years, and gradually a number of these accumulate, and for some reason all may materialize simultaneously and abnormally swell the total of building operations.

Together, Holabird and Roche worked as a close-knit team. Holabird, who took care of business, often dominated, but Roche, the designer, stood up for himself if he thought he was right, Renwick observed. "They were very fond of each other," Renwick wrote. "Holabird would sometimes lose patience with Roche and cuss him out around the office, yet behind it all he thought the world of him."

**THE MONROE BUILDING WAS BUILT BY THE GEORGE A. FULLER COMPANY,** which was hired in February 1911, three months after the building was announced. The company was another key player in the development of the Chicago style of commercial architecture. Like the Brooks brothers, Aldis, Holabird, and Roche, George Fuller made tall buildings possible. Although he died in 1900, his company continued to use the unique building techniques he established when he moved to Chicago in 1880. Wrote Renwick:

GEORGE FULLER

> He was a man of sterling honesty, and had a grip of building construction which made him one of the outstanding figures among contractors of that period. He was closemouthed, had not many friends, attentive to business, constantly using methods unknown to the older buildings. He was particularly keen on the assembling of materials. Right at the start he made a record for speed better than anything that had been done. Fuller also made a strenuous effort to operate under cost and percentage. He hoped to show that by careful buying, painstaking guidance of the work and securing the intelligent cooperation of subordinate contractors, he could put up a building on a cost-plus basis cheaper than at a fixed price. He did.

Fuller, too, was born in the East, in Templeton, Massachusetts, about sixty miles west of Boston. He studied architecture at the Boston School of Technology and took a job at the prominent Boston firm of Peabody & Stearns. He was assigned to work on mansions in Newport, Rhode Island, but was more interested in skyscrapers, so he moved to Chicago and worked as a general contracting partner. Two years later, at the age of thirty-one, he started the George A. Fuller Company, one of the first construction companies set up as a corporation.

"I'm a skyscraper man," Fuller told a friend. "Where you see a vacant lot or a hole in the ground, I see steel skeletons going up twenty, thirty, fifty stories in the air with people working and living in the clouds. I'm looking for men who can see the things I see—and for one man in particular who can see even higher and farther than I can."

It did not take long for Fuller to make his mark. In 1884, he won the contract for the Chicago Opera House. The grand theater, wrapped in a ten-story office tower, was described as the first "fireproof, steel constructed, electric lighted theatre in the country." What was even more unusual for the time was that all the building's construction was done under one contract.

"Fuller streamlined the whole process: a single bid for a single contract made a single firm entirely responsible, either through in-house expertise or subcontracts, for financing, demolition, site engineering, procurement of building materials, their timely arrival on site, and construction," wrote architectural historian Edward W. Wolner in his book *Henry Ives Cobb's Chicago.* Fuller soon established an impeccable reputation for scheduling work, ordering and staging material, organizing trades, and working with labor unions.

THE GEORGE A. FULLER COMPANY, WHICH BUILT THE MONROE BUILDING, CONSTRUCTED THE FLATIRON BUILDING IN NEW YORK CITY. THE BUILDING WAS ORIGINALLY KNOWN AS THE FULLER BUILDING BECAUSE THAT IS WHERE THE FIRM MOVED ITS HEADQUARTERS IN 1902.

THE FULLER COMPANY WAS KNOWN FOR ITS METAL-FRAME CONSTRUCTION IN PLACES LIKE NEW YORK'S PENN STATION, WHICH OPENED IN 1910. THE ENGINEERING FIRM OF PURDY & HENDERSON, A LATER TENANT IN THE MONROE BUILDING, DESIGNED THE CONCOURSE.

As builder William A. Starrett, brother of Paul Starrett and the author of *Skyscrapers and the Men Who Build Them,* noted, Fuller refashioned the building trades:

> Contractors until the mid to late 1880s usually had been boss carpenters or masons, men of little capital and foremanship, with little technical education, who executed sub-contracts under the supervision of architects. As buildings grew in complexity architects were overwhelmed with the multiplicity of burdens for which many of them had little training and no aptitude. Fuller raised contracting from a limited trade to both an industry and a profession, visualizing the building problem in its entirety—promotion, finance, engineering, labor and materials; and the architect reverted to his original function of design. Fuller first was a salesman who sought out property owners and promoted new buildings; secondly, an expert who understood the income possibilities and necessities of office buildings; then a financier who arranged the capital and; next an engineer competent to oversee every phase of modern building; and lastly, a business executive, buying and assembling materials to the best advantage and commanding a staff of assistants and an army of subcontractors and laborers.

Fuller worked with Holabird & Roche on the Tacoma and Pontiac Buildings and with Burnham & Root on The Rookery and the Rand McNally Building (1890) and built both halves of the Monadnock Building. His impact went beyond his organizational skills. Fuller was an early proponent of using steel instead of cast iron in supporting tall buildings. It was with the Chicago Opera House that he first employed steel floor beams to connect to cast-iron columns. Soon he was using steel exclusively, relying on electric hoists to haul beams into place and figuring out new ways—red-hot rivets instead of bolts—to fasten the steel together. Steel replaced cast iron because it could be tested and because it could be fastened more easily, Fuller told a reporter. It made it possible to build tall buildings that were light, strong, and safe.

"Mr. Fuller was the poet or the romancer of steel beams," observed the *Tribune* in 1900. "How daring was the flight of fancy which first imagined a cobweb structure of thin steel girders towering up 250 feet into the air without the support of heavy stone walls may be realized any day by the layman who watches a skyscraper in process of construction."

The same year, the authors of *A History of the City of Chicago: Its Men and Institutions* declared: "No other firm in the world perhaps has played so large a part in this revolutionizing the building trade as the George A. Fuller Company. And to them primarily is due the credit of having originated many of the actual construction methods now in general use." More than a century later, architectural historian Robert Bruegmann agreed; Fuller's work, he said, "revolutionized large-scale construction around the country."

Fuller's company grew rapidly during the first decades of the twentieth century. Having built six hundred buildings between 1900 and 1914, it was the logical choice in 1911 to construct the Monroe Building.

**IT TOOK A VILLAGE TO FASHION THE SIXTEEN-STORY SKYSCRAPER** at 104 South Michigan Avenue. From the first floor to the roof, it was a rare mix of artistry and emerging technology. Crews constructed the building, sculptors crafted its terra-cotta facades, and potters lathered its ceramic lobby—all in a matter of months.

The Monroe was Order 118 in 1911 for the Northwestern Terra Cotta Company, which clad the building's two street-facing facades above the second floor in a terra cotta that the company called Standard Granite because it was made to look like stone. With red and gray speckles embedded in the terra-cotta bisque, the color of the cladding varied slightly. The horizontal course of terra cotta alternated between appearing a bit more red or gray, creating a unique subtle banding pattern on the building. "It looked tutti-frutti ice cream," said Bruegmann.

Northwestern Terra Cotta, like the George A. Fuller Company and Holabird & Roche, was at its prime when the Monroe Building was constructed. Founded in the years just after the Great Chicago Fire, Northwestern had perfected clay chemistry and prided itself on making the highest grades of architectural terra cotta. Although the firm was incredibly busy (an advertisement mentioned sixteen prominent Chicago buildings the firm was working on—including the Monroe—in 1911), it could be counted on to manufacture and deliver work on schedule.

Terra cotta was the perfect material to cover the metal frames of the new skyscrapers. It was pliant in the making and durable after being fired in a kiln. Architects soon learned that this strange mix of clay, grog (already-fired clay), chemicals, and minerals could fireproof and protect their steel structures inexpensively and effectively. Terra cotta was cheaper and lighter than masonry, could be easily lifted and fitted into place, and lent itself to being shaped into ornament by skilled craftsmen. Terra cotta gussied up the stark new architecture of the Chicago School and looked just like stone. "It is indestructible and as hard and as smooth as any porcelain ware," noted *The Economist.* "It will be washed by every rainstorm and may if necessary be scrubbed like a dinner plate."

That is why the turn of the century was the age of terra cotta. The use of the material doubled during the 1890s and quadrupled during the first dozen years of the new century. By 1913, Northwestern Terra Cotta Company was the nation's largest supplier. It employed fifteen hundred workers at a twenty-four-acre factory complex on Chicago's North Side accessible by a street that is still known as Terra Cotta Place.

In Italian, *terra cotta* means "baked earth," and it has been around for thousands of years. Terra cotta that was hardened by fire or simply dried in the sun was one of the earliest materials used to make sculpture. From Mexico to Egypt to China, idols and figurines were sculpted out of the clay. In ancient Greece, figurines were molded in terra cotta, some of the first mass-produced products ever made.

It was the early Greeks and Romans who started using terra cotta on

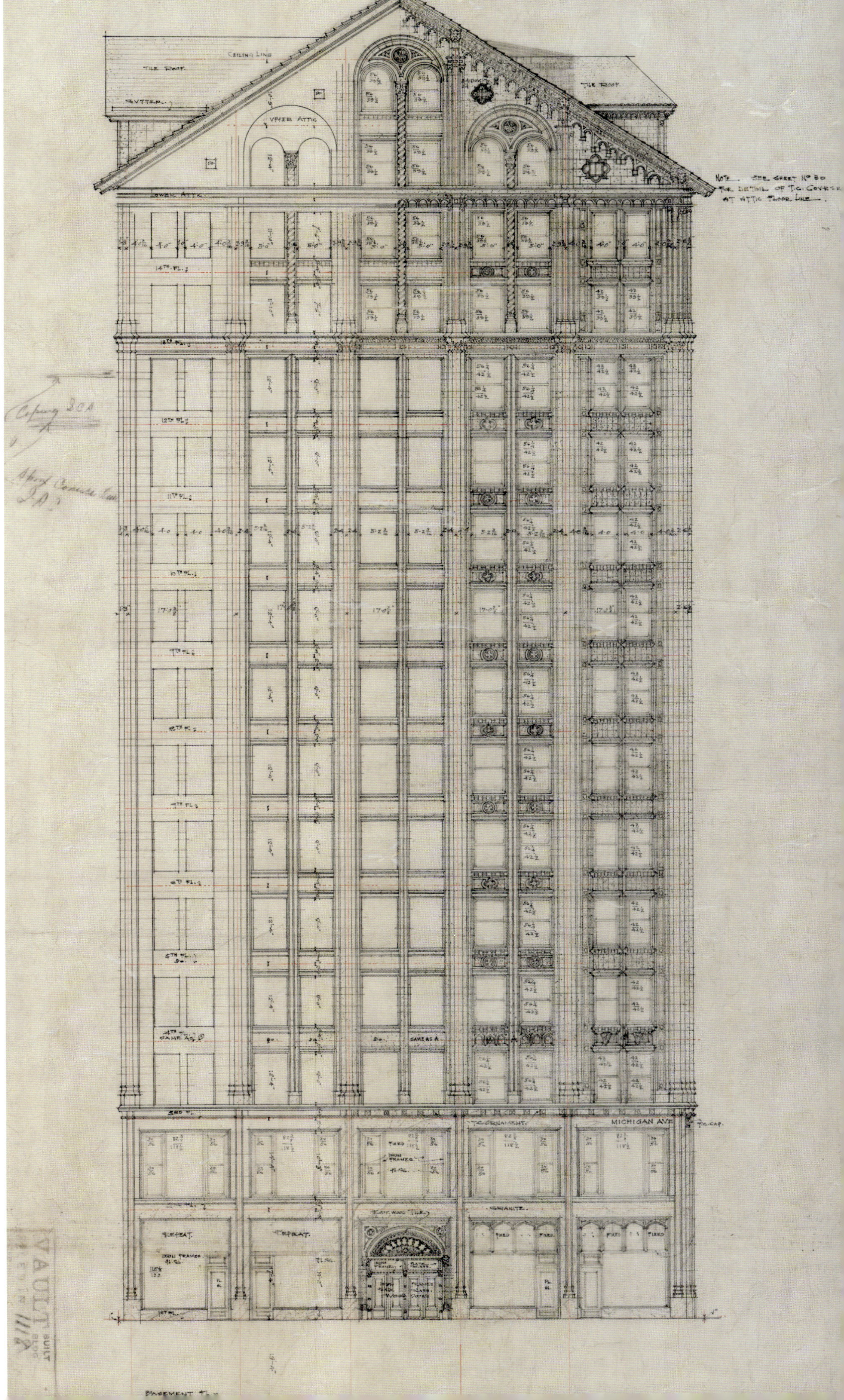

DRAWING SHOWS THE FRONT OF THE MONROE BUILDING. THE TWO-STORY BASE OF THE BUILDING WAS CLAD IN LIMESTONE. THE UPPER FOURTEEN-STORY FACADES ON MICHIGAN AVENUE AND MONROE STREET WERE COVERED IN TERRA COTTA.

WORKERS AT THE NORTHWESTERN TERRA COTTA COMPANY IN 1912, THE YEAR THE MONROE BUILDING OPENED. THE COMPANY'S FACTORY WAS ABOUT FIVE MILES NORTHWEST OF THE MONROE.

structures. They used the fired clay for roofs and columns and to decorate capitals, moldings, and pilasters on structures situated far from marble supplies. Architectural terra cotta has gone in and out of style; it experienced a revival in Germany and England in the mid-1800s and soon after in the United States.

"Over twenty centuries of use testify that the durability of burned clay is unexcelled by any other known material," proclaimed a Northwestern brochure in 1928. "Terra cotta reliefs from Nineveh, Babylon, Egypt, and ancient Greece, bear witness to this fact. World-famed buildings of the early Renaissance in Italy also show today practically no deterioration of the terra cotta."

Northwestern pioneered the manufacture of architectural terra cotta. The company was founded by Gustav Hottinger, who came to Chicago from Vienna at twenty-one. He studied modeling and sculpture at the Chicago Academy of Fine Arts and was then hired by the Chicago Terra Cotta Works. In 1878, he and two partners put up a thousand dollars each to start a rival terra-cotta company with six employees that would eventually be known as Northwestern. The fire of 1871 provided Northwestern with a substantial customer base because Chicagoans were intent on rebuilding their downtown all at once. Stone carvers could not keep up with the demand for keystones and lintels, and architects soon turned to the terra-cotta makers. By the turn

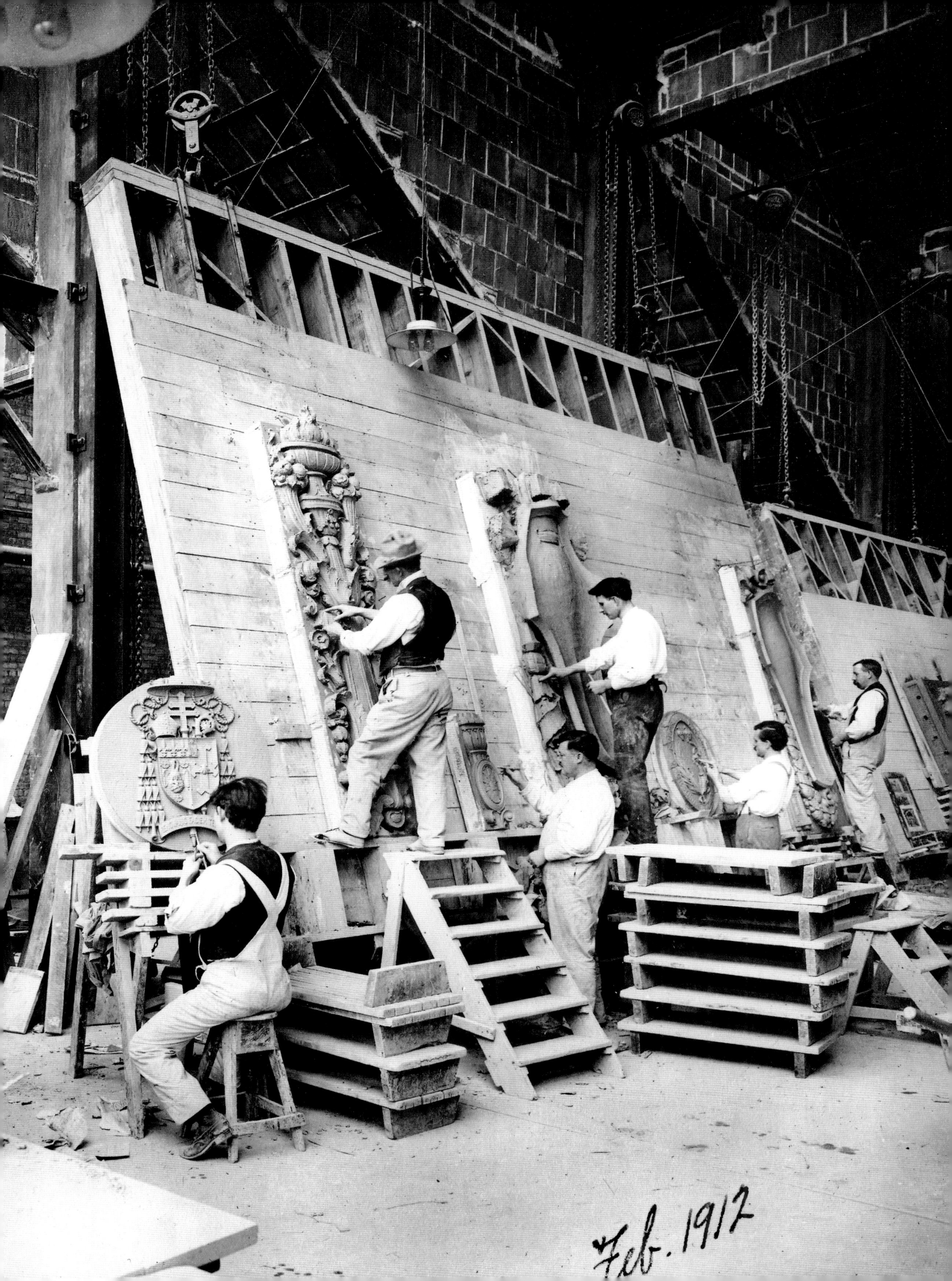
Feb. 1912

1'-10 7/16"
1'-6 13/32
EST END OF ORNAMENT UNDER NORTH EAVES
2'-0 13/16"
EAST CORNER OF ORNAMENT-0 13/16"
ED BORDER UNDER SOUTH
EAVES · EAST END OF
BORDER UNDER NORTH EAVES
THE SAME REVERSED
1'-6 21/32
11"
2'-0 13/16
SOUTH END OF EAST
GABLE; NORTH END OF WEST
GABLE THE SAME. NORTH END OF
EAST AND SOUTH END OF WEST THE
SAME REVERSED

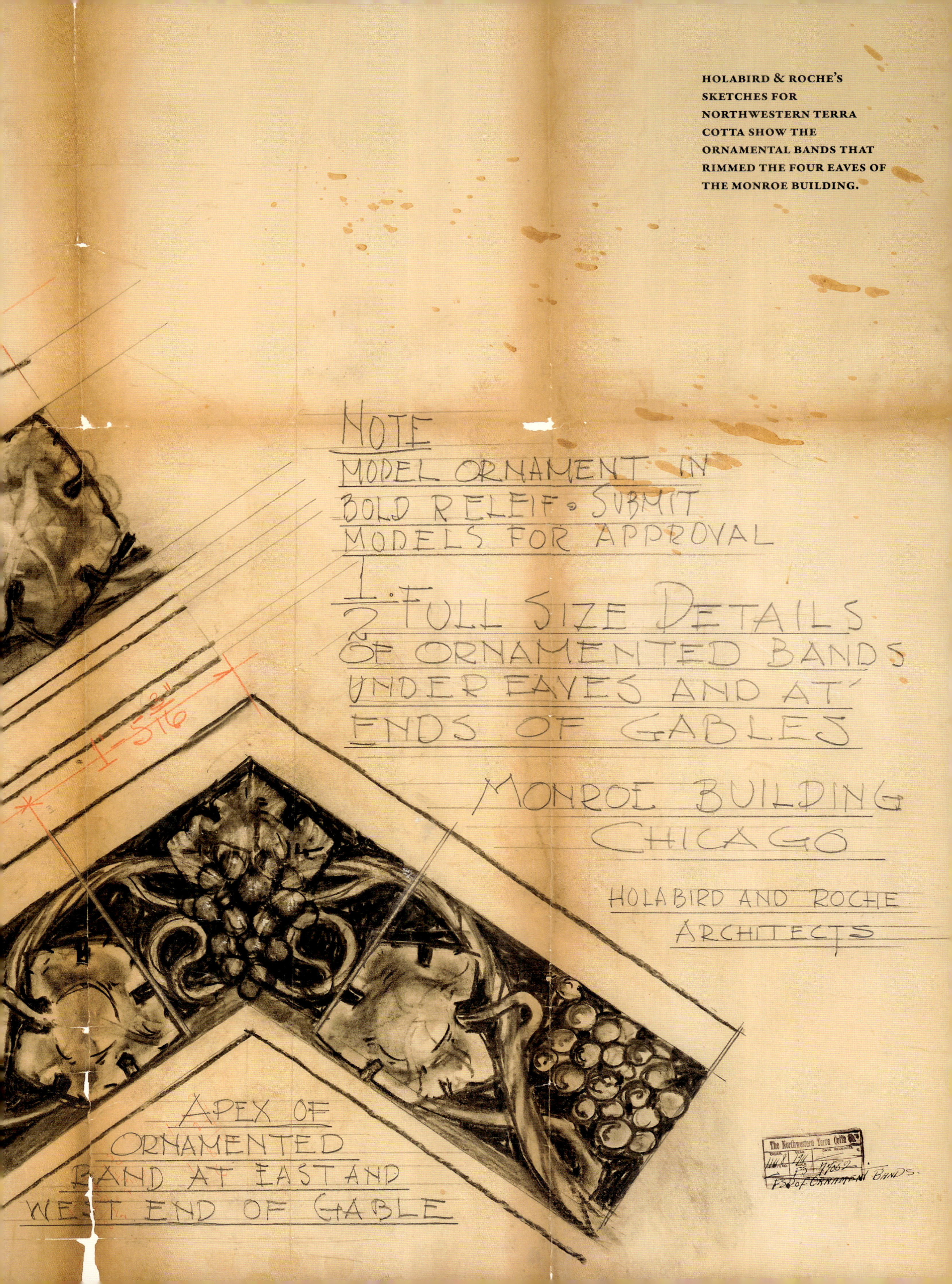


**HOLABIRD & ROCHE'S SKETCHES FOR NORTHWESTERN TERRA COTTA SHOW THE ORNAMENTAL BANDS THAT RIMMED THE FOUR EAVES OF THE MONROE BUILDING.**

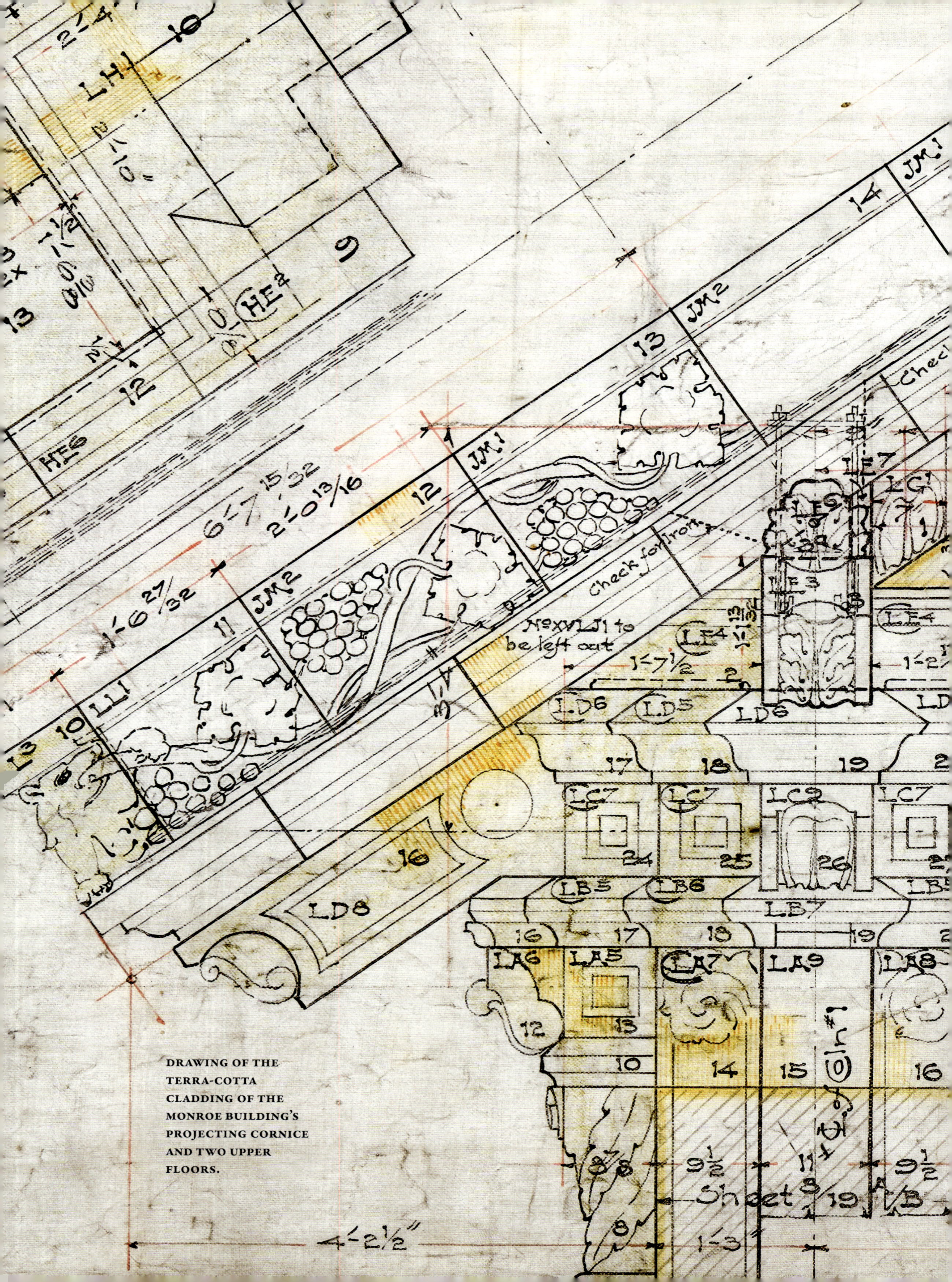

DRAWING OF THE TERRA-COTTA CLADDING OF THE MONROE BUILDING'S PROJECTING CORNICE AND TWO UPPER FLOORS.

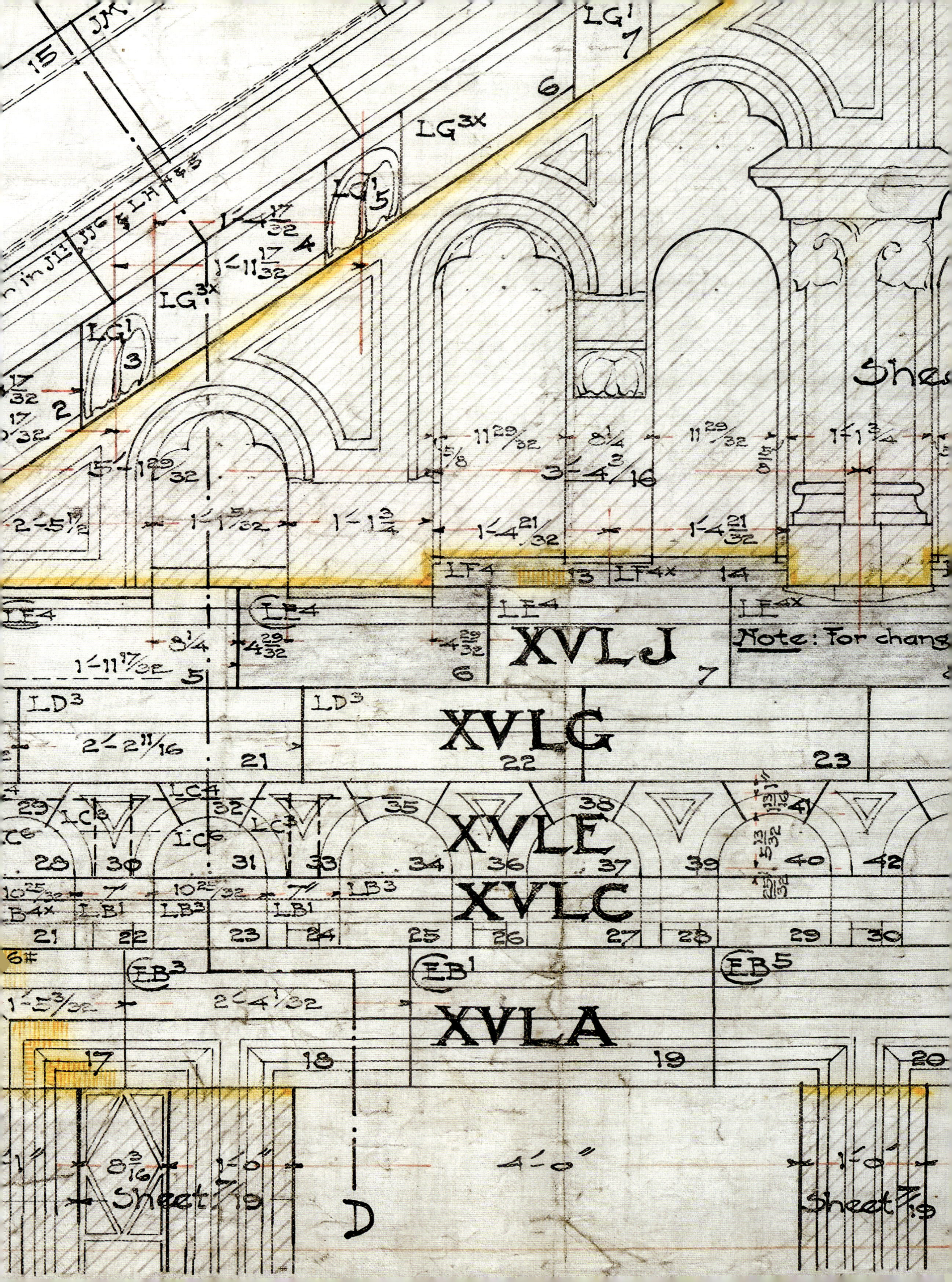

XVLJ
XVLG
XVLE
XVLC
XVLA
Note: For chang
Sheet 7/19
Sheet 7/19
D

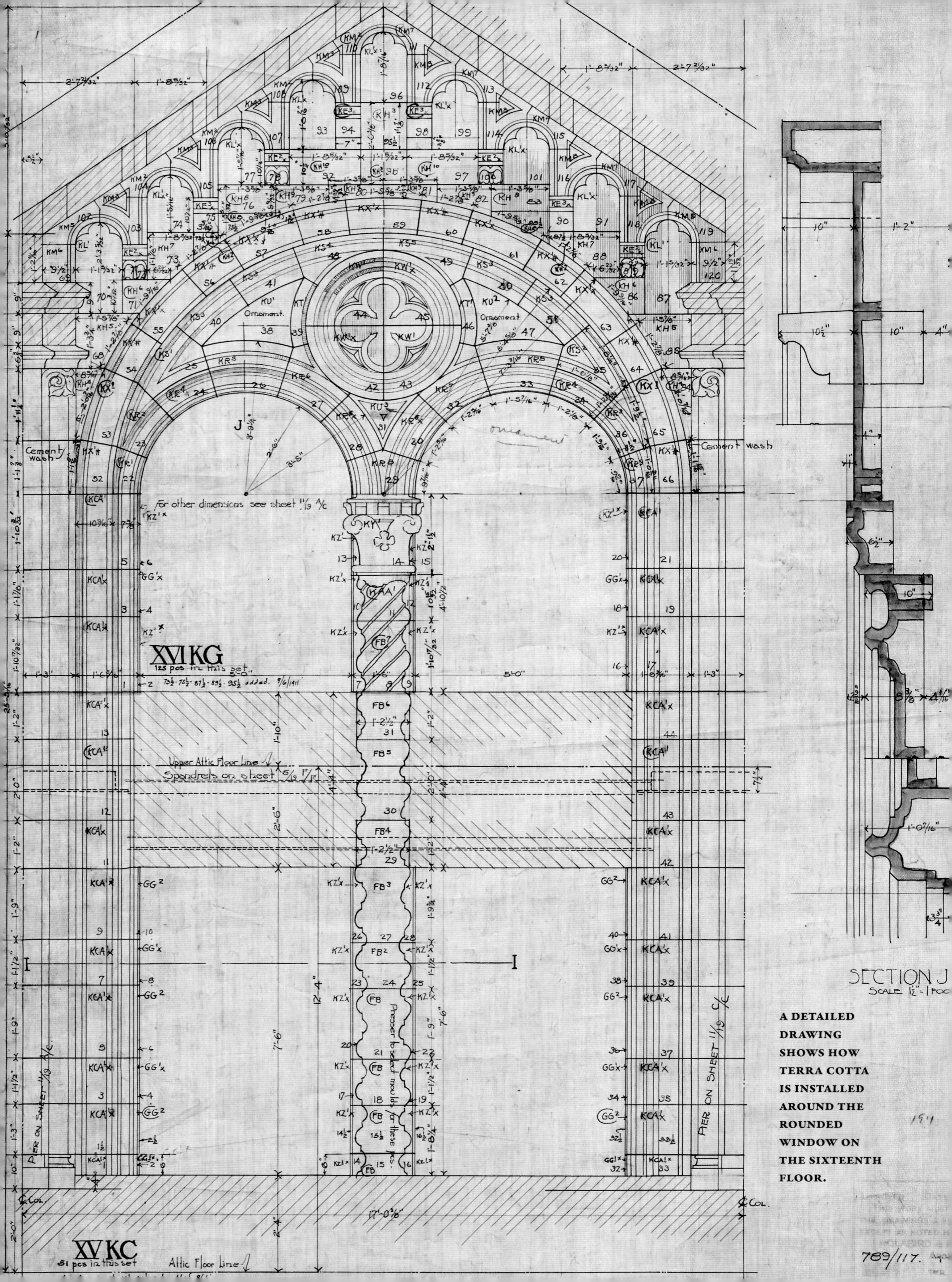


A DETAILED DRAWING SHOWS HOW TERRA COTTA IS INSTALLED AROUND THE ROUNDED WINDOW ON THE SIXTEENTH FLOOR.

of the century, Northwestern would be cladding entire skyscrapers in terra cotta.

Northwestern's terra cotta created a city of color. W. W. Boyington chose a pink finish for the Columbus Memorial Building and D. H. Burnham & Company picked a green glaze for the Stewart Building. Architects used an enameled cream-tinted terra cotta for the Railway Exchange Building and the Mandel Brothers Store, an enameled white for the Republic and Reliance Buildings, and an enameled dull white for the Schlesinger & Mayer department store, which soon became known as the Carson Pirie Scott store.

But as the years passed, the original color was of little importance. "Glazed terra cotta offers the greatest resistance to the accumulation of grime upon building surfaces," Northwestern bragged, "and the further advantage that cleaning is accomplished thoroughly and economically with plain soap and water." But the owners of most terra-cotta building could not keep up with the smoke and grit that twentieth-century industrial Chicago produced. The multi-colored Monroe Building darkened.

**THE PROCESS OF MANUFACTURING TERRA COTTA FOR FACADES** was exhaustive, involving dozens of men and several months.

To start, a Northwestern estimator worked with the architect to calculate how many square feet were to be faced with terra cotta. He figured out how many custom molds would be needed. Then a ceramist estimated how much glaze would be required to add color and finish. Next a draftsman made detailed shop drawings on linen or kraft paper. Sometimes he produced full-size drawings of details, making sure the sketches were slightly larger than the finished product because the terra cotta would shrink by 8 percent when fired.

Clay was modeled at this slightly larger size and used to create plaster molds. "The production of objects in terra-cotta from models and reproduction from casts are chiefly mechanical, but oftentimes call for experience and skill," warned Charles Thomas Davis in his 1884 guide *A Practical Treatise on the Manufacture of Bricks, Tiles, Terra Cotta, Etc.*

The terra cotta made at Northwestern was a mixture of clay from many sources fused with grog for strength and with chemicals for coloring. It was pressed by hand or with beaters into the plaster molds and then hollowed out to make it lighter and easier to attach to buildings.

"The making of moulds for terra-cotta, when the design is intricate, is a matter of great nicety, and requires careful fittings of the parts, which is not always easy, from the shrinking of the parts not being the same," Davis wrote.

The cooling process, too, was tricky: "When the shaped clay is withdrawn from the mould, it is usually dried by exposure to the sun or air, or near the hot kilns; but none of these methods are proper, as a greater uniformity of drying is absolutely necessary for moulded terra-cotta of all classes."

A special drying room was needed, with heat supplied from two furnaces placed at opposite ends. "The walls of this building should be of brick, and 'daubed;' or, commonly speaking, plastered on the inside with soft mud made from the loamy sand or washings found in gulleys and other places where it has been carried by water," he advised.

Once dried correctly, the terra cotta was fired in kilns at temperatures beyond two thousand degrees for 105 to 120 hours. It cooled for six days and was then trimmed, standardized, finished by hand, numbered, packed in straw to be transported the building site, and installed by masons.

Hottinger was able to direct his workers through this painstaking process day after day. He became an important part of the success of the Chicago School, working closely with the leading architects of the age. He supported Louis Sullivan by purchasing Sullivan's cottage in Ocean Springs, Mississippi, in 1910 when the architect fell upon hard times. Hottinger eventually became the sole owner of Northwestern. Upon his retirement in 1923, he divided his ownership interest in the company, worth between $2 million and $4 million, among the six men who'd helped him launch the enterprise and thirty longtime employees.

"It long has been my wish to turn over to those old time faithful workers who started when the company was practically nothing, the concern which they have helped to make," he said. "The time has come when I want to rest."

**A MATERIAL SIMILAR TO TERRA COTTA** was used on the interior of the Monroe Building. The lobby's walls, floor, and vaulted ceiling are covered with intensely colored glazed ceramic tiles known as architectural faience. These decorative tiles give the entrance a gem-like quality—"It is a built-in museum of ceramic art," said Tim Samuelson—and make it clear that you have entered an Arts and Crafts treasure.

Faience (pronounced fay-AHNS) originated more than a thousand years ago with Middle Eastern artisans, who used tin oxide to create a glaze that became white, shiny, and opaque after firing. Smooth and perfect as fine china, the earthenware could be molded, decorated, and colored.

The process was revived many times by ceramists, including those in the Italian town of Faenza, where it got its name. But the faience in the Monroe's lobby has much closer origins. It was designed and crafted by the Rookwood Pottery Company in Cincinnati, Ohio. Rookwood, like the other firms, was at its peak when it was enlisted to help create the Monroe Building.

Rookwood is one of the country's oldest manufacturing companies founded by a woman. Maria Longworth Nichols Storer, the granddaughter and daughter of Cincinnati's most prominent businessman and arts patrons of the period, could well have been classified as a member of the idle rich when she assumed her place in society during the mid-nineteenth century. Born Maria Longworth, she took the name Nichols from her first marriage and the name Storer from her second. In 1873, the twenty-four-year-old borrowed

a set of china-painting colors from a neighbor and started reading about Japanese pottery, which stirred an interest in art. She studied ceramics at the Cincinnati University's school of design and displayed her china pottery in the Women's Pavilion at the Philadelphia Centennial Exhibition in 1876, the first world's fair in the United States. She was deeply impressed by the Japanese art and design she saw there.

"It was there that I first felt a desire to have a place of my own where things could be made; and I wanted to import a complete Japanese pottery, workmen and all," she later told *Art Journal*. "My father laughed at the impracticability of this undertaking when I proposed it to him, but the idea of my making pottery interested him." Storer—described as vivacious, attractive, and ambitious, with a "profound artistic sense"—was used to getting her way. In 1880, she opened a pottery studio on the banks of the Ohio River and called it Rookwood. It was officially named after her father's estate, but she particularly liked the name because it reminded her of the British pottery firm Wedgewood.

The studio had two purposes, idealistic and practical. She wanted to create a local industry that searched for beauty and to prove that it could pay

**ROOKWOOD POTTERY ATOP MOUNT ADAMS IN CINCINNATI, OHIO. THE HALF-TIMBERED BUILDINGS, CALLED "A CITY OF ART" IN *BRICK* MAGAZINE, LOOKS MORE LIKE A CRAFT HOUSE THAN A FACTORY WITH DESIGNS ON ITS CEMENT WALLS. THE BULGING CHIMNEYS ARE ACTUALLY KILN CHIMNEYS.**

ROOKWOOD ARCHITECTURAL FAIENCE TILE PRODUCED IN THE ARTS AND CRAFTS TRADITION. THE TILE HAS A WIDE RANGE OF COLOR AND FINE MAT GLAZE THAT, THE COMPANY NOTES, "PERMITS AN ENTIRELY NEW FREEDOM OF DECORATIVE HANDLING BOTH IN MODELING AND IN PAINTING."

for itself. "While my principal object is my own gratification, I hope to make the pottery pay expenses," she told the *Cincinnati Daily Gazette.*

The new studio, which looked like a large Swiss chalet, opened at the same time that two major art movements and a social movement were converging. The Arts and Crafts movement promoted traditional craftsmanship. The Aesthetic movement pushed for art and beauty in everyday life—art for art's sake. And the so-called cult of domesticity favored the idea of women taking on work in traditional feminine roles, such as making pottery. By 1881, a "china mania" had overtaken Cincinnati and many parts of Ohio. Wrote Mrs. Aaron F. Perry in *Harper's New Monthly Magazine:* "It is curious to see the wide range of age and conditions of life embraced in the ranks of the decorators of pottery: young girls twelve to fifteen years of age find a few hours a week from their school engagements to devote to over or underglaze work, or to the modeling of clay; and from this up, through all the less certain ages, till the grandmother stands confessed in cap and spectacles, no time of life is exempt from the fascinating contagion."

From the start, Rookwood experimented. It created new colored glazes, tints, and finishes and attempted original abstract designs. Storer intended Rookwood to produce new pottery of Ohio Valley clay and a style all its own. "The object was to make beautiful things out of the simplest materials," she said.

The result was artistic handmade products (the company boasted that each of its pieces was touched by at least twenty-one sets of hands) that were individual (initialed by artists) and unique. Its glazes were rich, but irregular and crackled or crazed. Within a few years, Rookwood had altered the idea that pottery must be perfect.

People noticed. Rookwood's handmade and hand-painted pottery, tile, and teapots were expensive but in demand. Just a few years after Rookwood opened, C. Hennecke & Company gloated in a Christmas advertisement that it was the Chicago agent for Rookwood pottery. The next year, Burley & Company China and Glass advertised that its State Street store carried Rookwood. "We are now opening the handsomest collection of this Ware ever displayed in the city. The beauty of its somber colors and highly fashioned glaze is in striking contrast with the present general character of Ornamental Wares. It is advisable to see it while the assortment is complete."

Rookwood won a gold medal at the world's fair in Paris in 1889, beating out 615 ceramics exhibitors. In 1893, it received the "highest award" at the World's Columbian Exposition in Chicago. Wrote the *Chicago Tribune:* "Turn to the beautiful Rookwood pottery, born in the brain of Mrs. Bellamy Storer of Cincinnati, and admit that woman has created a rare art industry."

After the turn of the century, Rookwood expanded its product line and created an architectural department. For two decades, the company prided itself on turning out individual pieces as an art studio rather than a factory. But in 1903, Rookwood officials decided they would use the company's ceramics expertise to make architectural faience for walls (both interior and exterior), floors, and ceilings. Most of the work was custom-made, but Rookwood also sold stock pieces.

The company's first major order was creating tiles for the New York subway system—including a depiction of the *Clermont,* Robert Fulton's steamboat, at the Fulton Street station and a large plaque at the Wall Street station.

Although faience was more expensive than terra cotta because it required a second kiln firing, it added color, texture, and shape to interior walls. And with its matte glaze, it was easy to keep clean.

"The most notable thing about faience is not only the much greater range of colors it offers than terra cotta, but the presence in these colors of that indefinable something which we call 'quality,'" wrote Rookwood's Sturgis Lawrence in a 1907 issue of *The Architectural Record.* The colors produced by Rookwood were brilliant, but they also maintained a subtle delicacy. That's because, Lawrence explained, the company placed its confidence in the potters and artisans who created the faience: "The widest latitude was allowed among the workers for individual artistic expression in the pottery and decorative specialties produced."

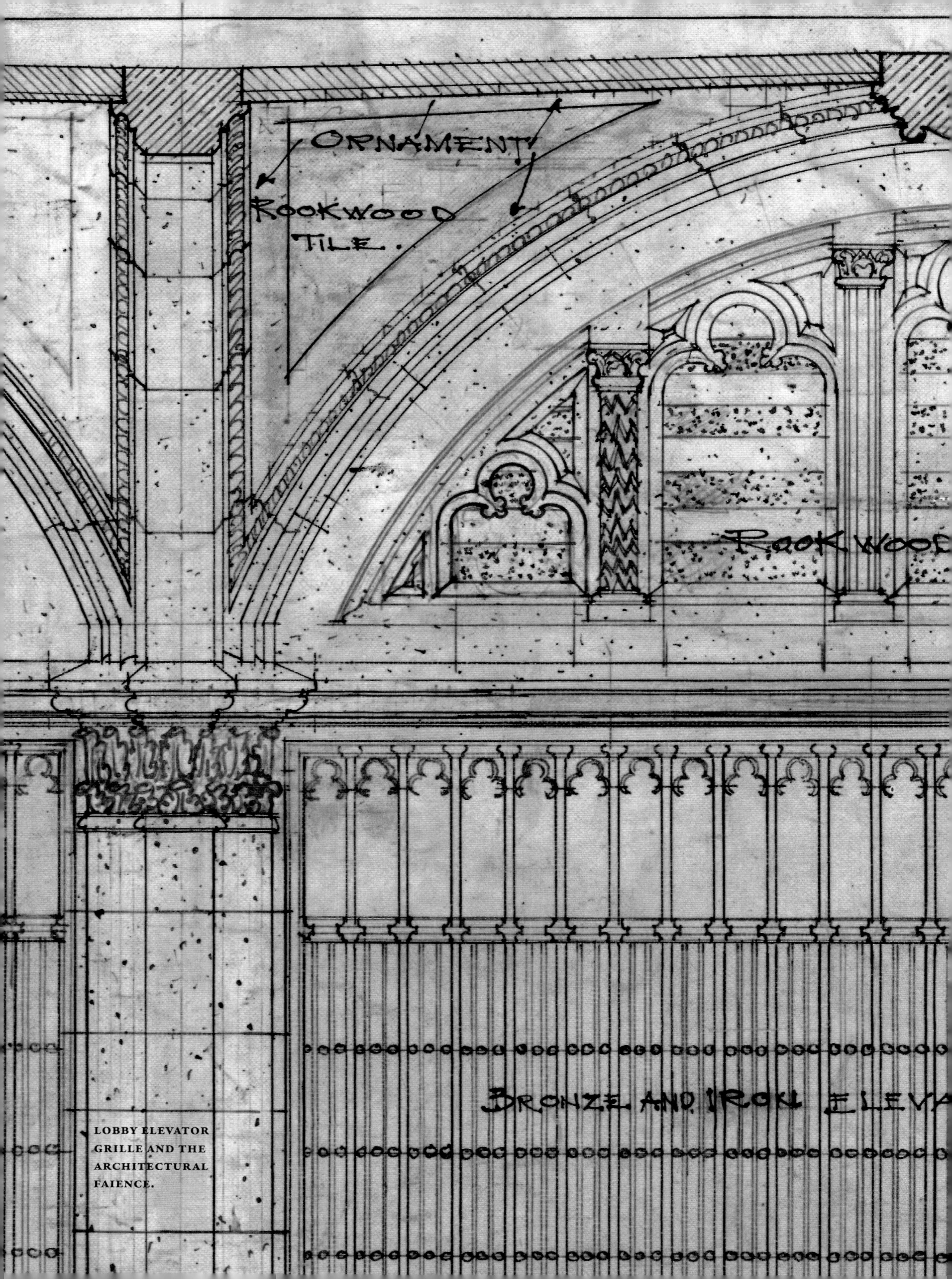


LOBBY ELEVATOR GRILLE AND THE ARCHITECTURAL FAIENCE.

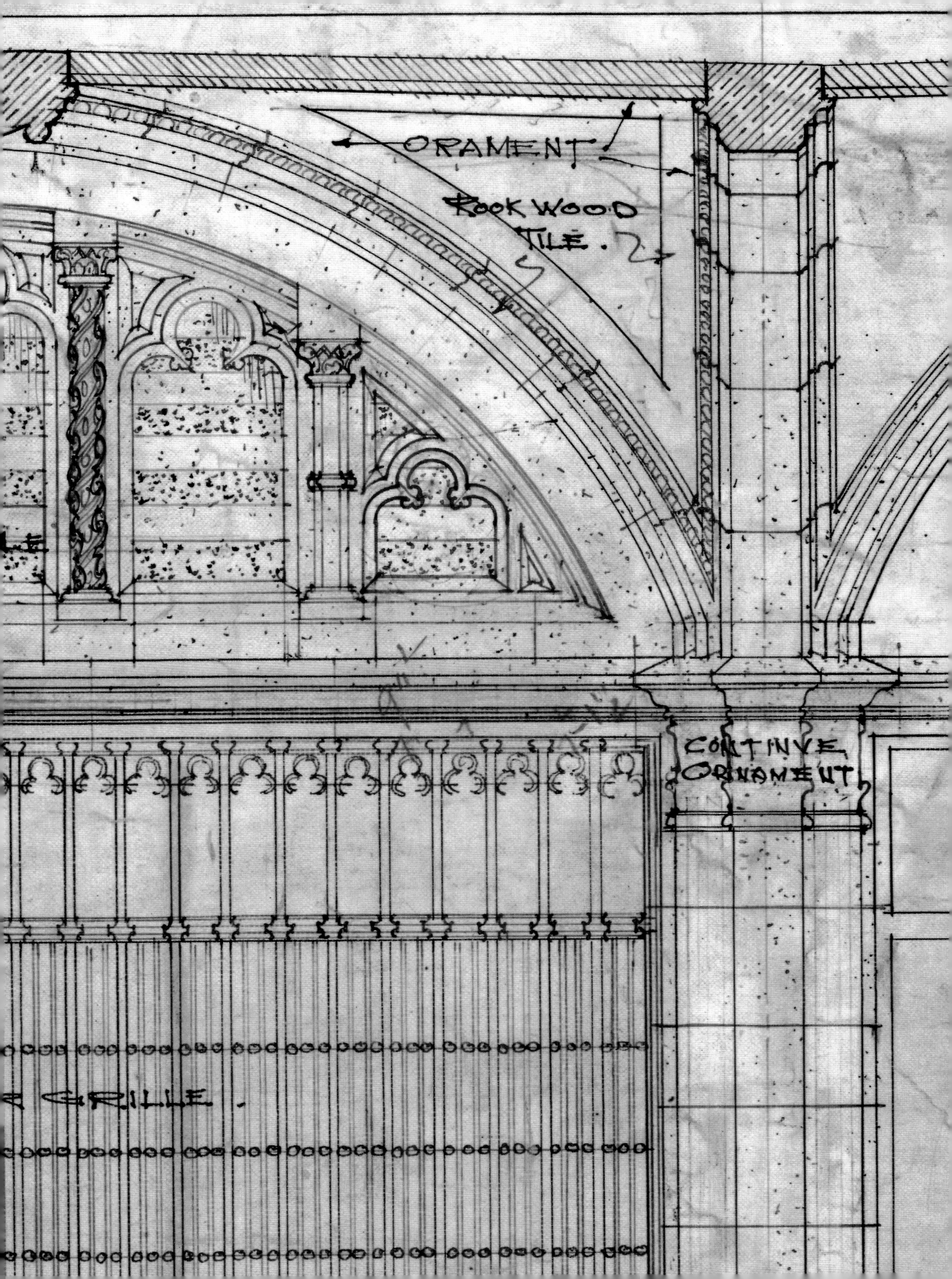
ORAMENT
ROOKWOOD
TILE.
CONTINVE
ORNAMENT
GRILLE.

Rockwood's architectural tiles were based on more than two thousand trials for color and quality of color. "This accumulated technical knowledge has been turned into the production of a colored glazed material for architectural use," Lawrence wrote. "To the extent that this may illustrate in varying degree the course of development among the present American manufacturers, it may be said that the material they are now offering the architect for the execution of his special designs represents the accumulated experience of a staff of highly trained artist-craftsmen working in close association with scientific technicians who have created their own precedents in the technology of ceramics."

The company went on to complete dozens of major commissions in hotels, restaurants, mansions, and churches. It created a tile version of the U.S. Department of the Treasury seal for the Treasury secretary's office in Washington, D.C., and did installations at Grand Central Station, the Forty-first Precinct police station in New York City, and in the rathskeller at the Seelbach Hotel in Louisville, Kentucky.

Rookwood's 1907 catalog warned potential customers that its architectural faience was made by hand and could not be hurried. "The shortest time for manufacture is three weeks, while more elaborate projects range from five weeks upward," the company cautioned. "If any disaster occurs in any stage of the process the material has sometimes to be refired, but more frequently made over from the start. These time requirements for the necessary processes and these risks of further delay from accidents are inseparable from a product which must go through fires at very high temperatures. They should be allowed for, because fine workmanship and individuality cannot be had without them. No cancellations after order started."

Over the years, Holabird & Roche brought Rockwood employees to Chicago to work on four projects: the Palm and German Rooms of the La Salle Hotel, the interior walls of the Brooks Building, the restaurant walls of the North American Building, and the Monroe Building.

Owen Aldis was convinced that an attractive lobby would attract top-quality tenants. He needed a lobby that could be easily washed, that did not have to be repainted, that was impervious to smoke and soot. He wanted to build something that was timeless. Something that was not dictated by a particular architectural style. He was artistic and practical. He didn't want to have to update the lobby over the years.

It is unclear from the architectural drawings how much of the design was Rookwood's, but the company's expertise is certainly evident in the execution of the lobby ornamentation of the Monroe Building.

**TWO DOZEN CONSTRUCTION PHOTOS SHOW HOW QUICKLY** the George A. Fuller Company worked. Using the most primitive of tools, it demolished the glass-fronted two-story building on Michigan Avenue and Monroe Street and built a new sixteen-story one in less than a year. To do that kind of work now

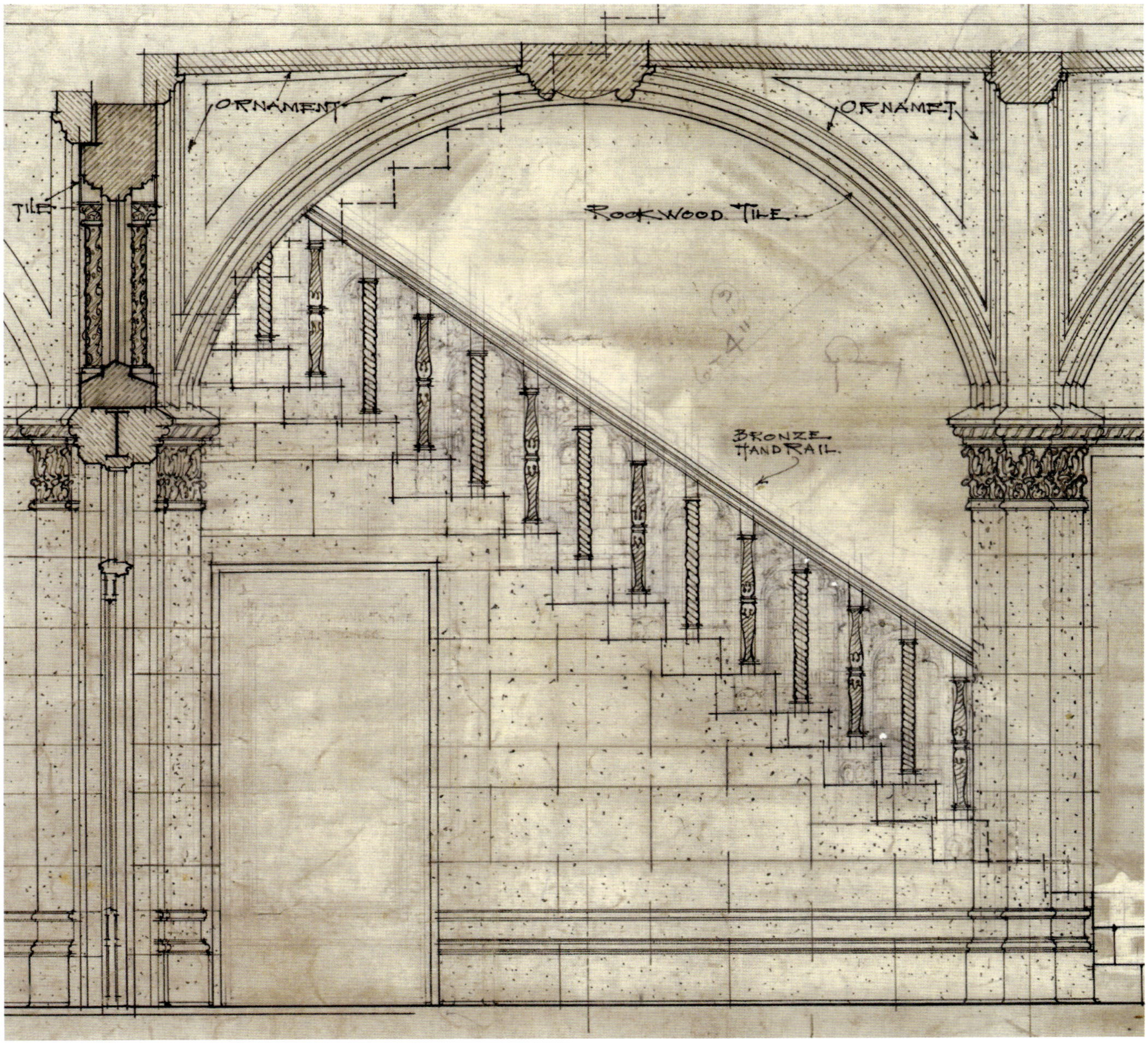


in the Loop, with much more powerful equipment, would likely take several years.

The first photo, which is undated but was probably taken in the early spring of 1911, shows the two-story building being razed as the site is cleared at grade. Billboards advertising actress Rose Stahl in the play *Maggie Pepper* are seen plastered on the side of the neighboring Illinois Athletic Club, at 112 Michigan Avenue. The play, which opened in early March, received tepid reviews from the *Tribune's* Percy Hammond, who pronounced: "'Maggie Pepper' is one of those baffling entertainments in the consideration of which the informative critic is madly tossed between desire and duty." The play lasted through June at the Illinois Theater.

By the time the photo dated May 26 was taken, one of the *Maggie Pepper*

**ARCHITECTURAL RENDERING OF THE MONROE BUILDING LOBBY. ARCHITECTS WORKED WITH ROOKWOOD POTTERY IN SPECIFYING WHERE TILE AND ORNAMENT WOULD BE PLACED.**

MONROE BUILDING SITE BEFORE DEMOLITION. . .

signs had been covered over by a billboard promoting Ethel Barrymore in *Alice-Sit-by-the-Fire* at the Blackstone Theater. (Hammond liked this play much better.) The photo shows a puny steam shovel excavating the basement and a horse-drawn loader waiting for debris. It is apparent from how many coats are hung on a wall that much of the work was being done by hand.

By June, a perimeter wall surrounding the site and signs proclaiming that George A. Fuller Company builders were at work indicated a new seriousness of purpose. Laborers had shored up the site and installed toolsheds and auxiliary lighting. Pile drivers had been brought in to sink deep holes that would be filled with "Chicago caissons," or cylindrical concrete piers to the hardpan below. Several photos show that the builders had brought in tarps to protect their excavation work from the elements.

...AND AFTER IN 1911.

Little evidence of progress could be seen again until late July, when an ancient-looking hoist was delivered. It was used to lift two-story steel beams vertically into position so they could be attached to the concrete caissons. The first beams can be seen in the July 21 photo. A week later, around a dozen beams were in place, and the steel framing of each floor was about to take off. By August 4, the framing of half the first floor was completed. Eight days later, workers had reached the third floor and started floor construction. By August 25, they were on the fifth floor. Here is when the work began to go so quickly that the pictures seem almost animated. By early September, workers were up to the eleventh floor. Late that month, they had reached the sixteenth floor. By early October, the entire building was framed.

The cladding proceeded even more quickly. Granite was installed on the first two floors in September, and terra-cotta work began later that month. It took only two months to clad the exterior of the building to the fourteenth floor. Installation of all the windows up to the gables, which began in early November, took less than a month. By January 1912, the building was nearly enclosed.

The Monroe, originally known as the Shepherd Brooks Building, according to an early advertisement, opened four months later and made the cover of the April 1912 issue of *The Architectural Record.* The accompanying article, which prominently featured the Monroe, illustrated the work of Holabird & Roche. "Undoubtedly there is such a thing as Chicago architecture, separable from architecture in Chicago," wrote critic Montgomery Schuyler (as Franz Winkler). "Even apart from the modern and unacademic performances of a few pioneers, the ordinary building of the ordinary architect in Chicago differs from the like building elsewhere, at least to the Eastward."

Not only were Chicago buildings tall, Schuyler pointed out, they were big and brawny and practical: "The Eastern man erecting an edifice for the use of his business feels in a manner bound to make it a proclamation of his commercial success. He willfully spends more money on it in the way of decoration, which so often does not decorate, than would be needed to accomplish its practical purpose." This was considered "mere nonsense" to pragmatic Chicago businessmen, Schuyler wrote. "In the judgment of the Chicagoan, the Easterner needs to 'scrap' a good deal of his academic learning," he continued. "Speaking of office buildings, the Westerner believes that the first function of every commercial building is to pay."

Schuyler focused on the work of Holabird & Roche because he admired the firm's "bare and untrained business building." He criticized some of the firm's projects, such as the North American Building, two blocks west of the Monroe, which didn't work for him because it appeared heavier at the top than the bottom. "Much more successful as objects of architecture than any of these are the two fronts on Michigan Avenue, of which one, the University Club, transcends the trammels of a business building, being in fact a club house, which not only admits but demands a more elaborate and domestic treatment than belongs to a strictly business building," he wrote. "The other, however, the Monroe Building, is strictly a business building and a very admirable example of its kind, having no more ornament than fairly expresses the structure."

Critic Harriet Monroe thought similarly about the two buildings. "Gothic design, by its emphasis upon vertical lines, would seem to lend itself more readily to skyscraping architecture," she wrote in the *Chicago Tribune* as the Monroe Building was opening. "In Chicago the University Club—a tall building though rather social than commercial in purpose—and the new Monroe building, both by Holabird & Roche, are admirable examples of successful and consistent use."

A sister-in-law and biographer of John Root, Monroe had a remarkably prescient view of Chicago architecture. She understood the originality of the

FOUNDATION CONSTRUCTION BEGAN IN THE SUMMER OF 1911.

SEQUENCE OF PHOTOS SHOWS MONROE BUILDING CONSTRUCTION. IT WAS FINISHED IN LESS THAN A YEAR.

new work and hailed its significance. She also figured out the major players, not an easy task in a city full of architectural geniuses:

> Of independent designers who reject the schools and orders, Chicago has a more interesting group than any other city. Back in the '80s John Root, though not quite a revolutionist, was a free thinker in architecture, as The Rookery and the northern Monadnock testify.
>
> Louis Sullivan had developed from the first his own ideas of design; the Gage and Carson, Pirie, Scott buildings show what beauty and symmetry may be achieved in a frank façade of iron, glass, and terra cotta, which borrows nothing from the old styles. These buildings are so brilliantly successful that the next age will undoubtedly reproach us for having so few of them.

Monroe also knew the importance of architecture.

"The public should be exacting in its demands and criticisms," she wrote. "The architects, more than any other artists of our age, are building an enduring monument. That it has imposing beauty and grandeur no one can deny who sees the Flatiron loom up over the crowded streets, or who walks down Michigan avenue while the lights come out, and the great buildings lose any casual defects of design as they rise loftily against the sky."

These were serious words.

"We should be jealous for this new art," she continued. "We should demand the utmost of our architects. For what the public demands it gets, and only when it demands great art is the most brilliant genius able to provide it."

**THE ORIGINAL RENTAL BROCHURE FOR THE MONROE BUILDING,** published by Aldis & Company, unabashedly pointed out the singularity of the property. "There is only one Michigan Avenue in Chicago, and there is not a more beautiful office building in the city than the Monroe Building," it proclaimed. Details like the double barrel vaulted lobby ceiling, the tile wainscoting in the corridors, the dark oak framing and mahogany sashes, and six high-speed elevators with flashlight signals were highlighted. "Each office will be provided with a cabinet for clothes and a lavatory with hot and cold water," the brochure stated. "On the second floor there will be a well-equipped barber shop, and there are toilets, both for men and women, on each floor, and a retiring room for women on the sixth floor."

The Rookwood tile was prominently mentioned, its use called "the first installation of this material on a large scale in a Chicago building." Although skyscrapers had been around for decades, the brochure made a point of assuring potential renters that the building was carefully constructed, stating: "The steel columns rest on concrete caissons extending down over 100 feet to bed-rock."

The Monroe Building opened in May 1912. *The Economist* noted early that month that streets surrounding the skyscraper were jammed with moving vans. "The Monroe Building has taken the cream of the tenants from a dozen

THE MONROE BUILDING IS MEANT TO HARMONIZE WITH THE UNIVERSITY CLUB OF CHICAGO AND CREATE AN EASTERN GATE TO CHICAGO'S DOWNTOWN ON MONROE STREET.

buildings and is not only an office structure but is full of shops for tailors and others," it reported. "The building is practically all occupied."

More than a hundred tenants filled the sixteen stories. As detailed previously in the *Tribune,* Capper & Capper took the most prominent first-floor space, along Michigan Avenue at the corner of Monroe Street. "It is a great 'Man's Store,' embracing every article of a man's wardrobe except his shoes," stated the announcement of its May 4 opening. The shoe store French, Shriner & Urner and Wood's Tea Shop, a holdover from the building that had previously occupied the site, rented the other Michigan Avenue retail spots. In September, the Cawston Ostrich Farm of South Pasadena, California, opened in the Monroe Street space. It sold genuine ostrich plumes, boas, fans, and novelties. "Get a Cawston Plume for Your Spring Hat," the firm advertised.

Like all downtown office buildings, the Monroe was a small city—with a barbershop, a nail salon, a stenographer's office, tailor shops, a stationery store, a pharmacy, and even a Christian Science reading room. The basement, the underbelly of that city, had three boilers, two coal rooms, and an ash room, as well as switchboards, a paint shop, a carpenter's shop, and a paper shop. Six elevators and a freight elevator ran up the fourteen floors, and stairs led to the two attic floors.

Most of the businesses that had offices in the Monroe—among them, the American Blueprint Company, the American Can Company, Mahin Advertising, and several small publishers—are now out of business. A few, such as the Great Lakes Dredge & Dock Company, the Ludowici-Celadon Company (now Ludowici Roof Tile), and Holabird & Roche (now Holabird & Root), are still in existence, though they now operate out of other buildings.

Downtown buildings often develop a certain culture. Those that are close to courthouses are filled with lawyers; those in the financial center attract brokers. But location does not define all buildings. For some reason, the nearby North American Building was filled with salesmen and suppliers who specialized in women's accessories. They sold leather goods, gloves, handkerchiefs, hosiery, handbags, scarves, and furs. The Monroe Building was known as a building for architects, artists, and physicians. "Designed for office purposes, the tenancy of the building will be confined to corporations, professional people and business firms of the highest standing," its sales brochure stated.

This professional air, as well as the unobstructed light along Michigan Avenue, drew doctors. The building's skylights fostered a creative spirit, attracting architects and artists, especially to the top two floors. The most prominent architect to lease in the Monroe was Frank Lloyd Wright, whose Chicago office was there in 1919. "Frank Lloyd Wright, Architect, 1600 Monroe Building" was how he marked the drawings for the never-built Shampay House in Chicago's Beverly neighborhood. The drawings were initialed by Rudolph Schindler, who ran Wright's Chicago office and Taliesin in Wisconsin while Wright was in Japan working on Tokyo's Imperial Hotel. Wright may also have designed the Irving House in Wilmette when his office was still in the Monroe Building, but the drawings were simply marked "Frank Lloyd Wright, Architect, Chicago."

The room that Wright's drawing referred to, 1600 Monroe Building, was first occupied by Walter Burley Griffin and then by Francis Barry Byrne; both architects worked for Wright in the early part of their careers. Griffin and his wife, architect Marion Mahony Griffin, created a large office on the sixteenth floor. Overlooking Michigan Avenue, it was called the attic because it was in the gable portion of the building. The space included a large drafting room beneath a skylight, three offices, a reception room, a display room, a studio, and a photo studio. The informal loft, reachable only by an ornamental staircase, attracted architects and artists. It was similar to a picturesque haven that existed in the unfinished truss space in the eleventh-floor attic of Steinway Hall, about three blocks south of the Monroe. There architects like Wright, the Griffins, and Dwight H. Perkins shared ideas and formed what became known as the Prairie School of Architecture.

Walter Griffin was still in his Steinway Hall office when he submitted plans for Canberra, the planned capital city of Australia, in an international competition. He received a telegram—"Your design awarded first place"—on May 23, 1912, just weeks after he moved into the Monroe. He stayed in the office for more than a year, refining his plan. Within a few years, Barry Byrne

MONROE BUILDING ENTRANCE ON MICHIGAN AVENUE AFTER THE ORIGINAL SWING DOORS WERE REPLACED BY REVOLVING DOORS.

ORIGINAL FRONT VESTIBULE OFF MICHIGAN AVENUE.

CUSTOM
TAILORS

THE BUILDING'S FIRST LOBBY. THIS PHOTO WAS ESSENTIAL IN PROVIDING CLUES TO RESTORE THE LOBBY SINCE THE BRONZE WALL FIXTURES AND ROOKWOOD TILE FLOOR WERE LONG GONE.

MARGARET AND ALFONSO IANNELLI IN THEIR MONROE BUILDING STUDIO IN 1915. THE MARRIED COUPLE WERE EARLY PROPONENTS OF MODERN ART IN EVERYDAY LIFE.

moved into Griffin's space and took over the commissions that Griffin had won but could not finish. Griffin moved to Australia in 1913, returning to the United States only for short periods. Byrne, too, spread the ideas of the Prairie School, creating modernist Catholic churches throughout the United States and Europe.

In 1915, Byrne subleased space to artists Alfonso and Margaret Iannelli, who stayed a year or two, producing sculpture and commercial art. Byrne also subleased the photo studio to Henry Fuermann, one of the first photographers to specialize in buildings and Louis Sullivan's favorite. During its first years in the Monroe Building, Henry Fuermann & Sons took detailed photographs of Wright's Midway Gardens, including pictures of Alfonso Iannelli's legendary sprite sculptures.

Artists like Hugh Stuart Campbell, who did pencil sketches of society women for the *Tribune* and early *Vogue* covers, and John Paulding, who sculpted World War memorials all over America, both maintained offices in smaller attic spaces. The largest attic office was occupied by Charles Daniel Frey, who started an "advertising art factory" to provide art and photography to

SPRITE SCULPTURES AT FRANK LLOYD WRIGHT'S MIDWAY GARDENS DESIGNED BY ALFONSO IANNELLI AND PHOTOGRAPHED BY MONROE BUILDING NEIGHBOR HENRY FUERMANN.

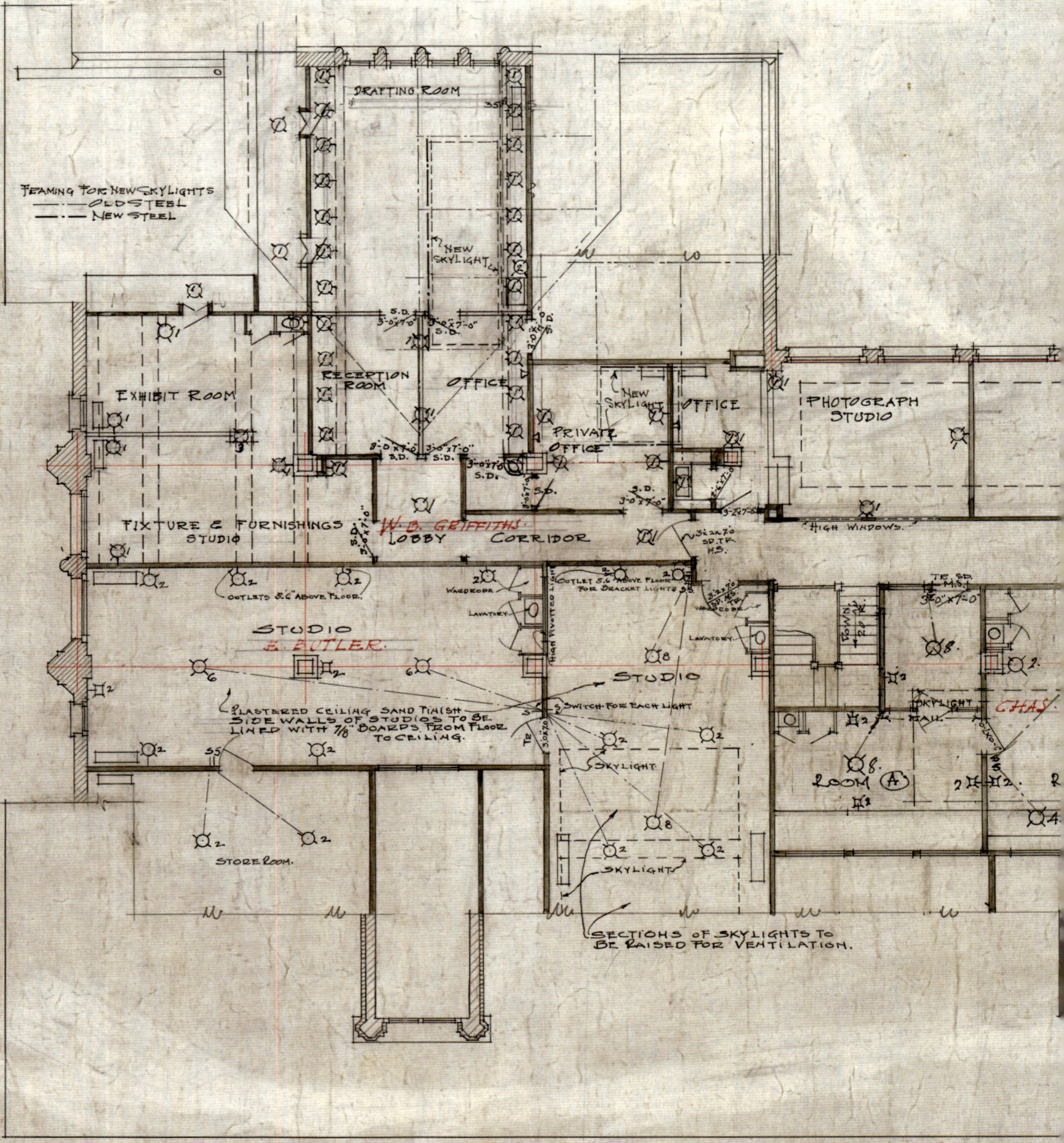

ORIGINAL PLAN FOR THE SIXTEENTH FLOOR. WALTER BURLEY GRIFFIN'S STUDIO FRONTED MICHIGAN AVENUE. THE OPEN SPACE AT THE TOP OF THE PLAN IS THE LIGHT COURT.

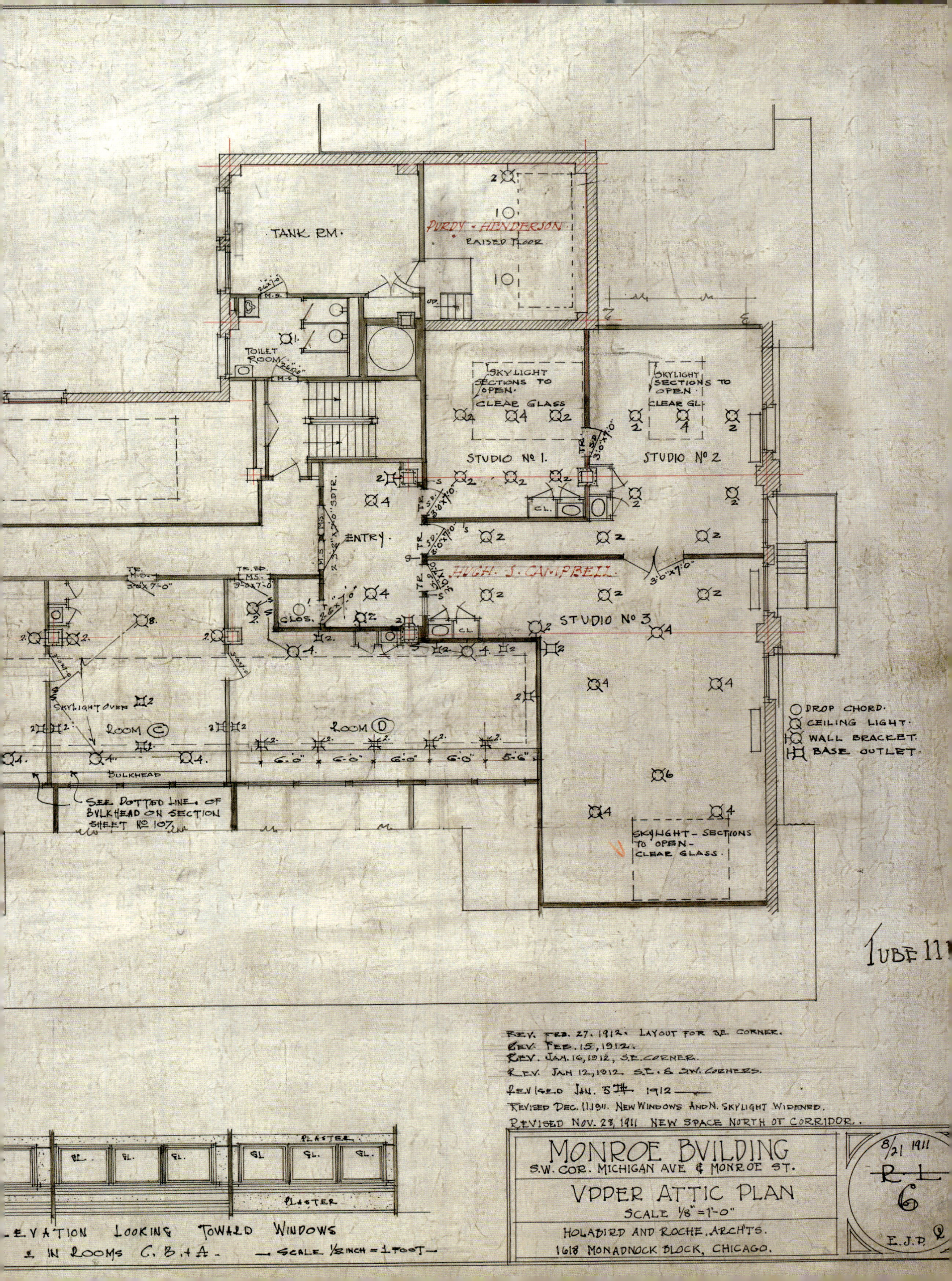
TANK RM.
PURDY · HENDERSON
RAISED FLOOR
TOILET ROOM
SKYLIGHT SECTIONS TO OPEN· CLEAR GLASS
SKYLIGHT SECTIONS TO OPEN· CLEAR GL.
STUDIO Nº 1.
STUDIO Nº 2
ENTRY.
HUGH S. CAMPBELL
CLOS.
CL.
STUDIO Nº 3
SKYLIGHT OVER
ROOM C
ROOM D
BULKHEAD
SEE DOTTED LINE OF BULKHEAD ON SECTION SHEET Nº 107
SKYLIGHT - SECTIONS TO OPEN - CLEAR GLASS.
DROP CHORD.
CEILING LIGHT.
WALL BRACKET.
BASE OUTLET.
TUBE 11
REV. FEB. 27. 1912. LAYOUT FOR S.E. CORNER.
REV. FEB. 15, 1912.
REV. JAN. 16, 1912, S.E. CORNER.
REV. JAN 12, 1912 S.E. & S.W. CORNERS.
REVISED JAN. 5TH 1912
REVISED DEC. 11 1911. NEW WINDOWS AND N. SKYLIGHT WIDENED.
REVISED NOV. 28, 1911 NEW SPACE NORTH OF CORRIDOR.
MONROE BUILDING
S.W. COR. MICHIGAN AVE & MONROE ST.
UPPER ATTIC PLAN
SCALE 1/8" = 1'-0"
HOLABIRD AND ROCHE. ARCH'TS.
1618 MONADNOCK BLOCK, CHICAGO.
8/21 1911
R 1
6
E.J.P.
PLASTER
GL.
ELEVATION LOOKING TOWARD WINDOWS IN ROOMS C, B & A. — SCALE 1/8 INCH = 1 FOOT —

ARCHITECT WALTER BURLEY GRIFFIN DESIGNED THE OFFICES OF P.F. VOLLAND COMPANY, THE FIRST PUBLISHERS OF RAGGEDY ANN AND RAGGEDY ANDY.

advertising companies. Frey's company produced drawings in every medium for magazines, newspapers, posters, books, catalogs, and announcements. "Originals in pen and ink, 'wash,' pencil, crayon, pastel and full oil color are here and there about the rooms—hand lettered pages, decorative initials and border designs, pictures of people doing things with every conceivable advertisable article," wrote Elbert Hubbard, an author and a publisher who visited the studios during the Monroe's early years. He found the place inspirational:

> Whenever I am in Chicago with an hour or two to spare, and feel the need of a mental bath, I go to the top floor of the Monroe Building and wander around through the beautiful, spacious, quiet offices and studios of Charles Daniel Frey. *The* Charles Daniel Frey *Company,* I should say, for Frey never allows the personal to take precedence over the *organization,* even with an intimate like me.
>
> Skylight is cold light, ordinarily—but up here under the gable of the Monroe Building, there is a tempering warmth in the gentle smile of welcome all through the place—from the sunny-haired girl at the switch-board to the chief.
>
> If it has been your privilege to visit the studios of artist free lances, the stroll through the Frey offices will be a revelation to you—and if you have, in your peregrinations, frequented the shop that we of the advertising craft call art factories, then this little journey is going to thrill you—by contrast.

BARRY BYRNE'S ARCHITECTURE STUDIO IN ROOM 1600. BYRNE WORKED WITH WALTER BURLEY GRIFFIN AFTER GRIFFIN MOVED TO AUSTRALIA TO DESIGN THE CITY OF CANBERRA.

Two decades later, the fledgling architectural firm of Skidmore & Owings (later Skidmore, Owings & Merrill) took over the sixteenth-floor offices. It would become one of the largest architectural and engineering firms in the world. The names of N. A. Owings and Louis Skidmore first showed up in the 1936–37 Monroe Building directory as occupying room 1601. John O. Merrill joined them in the 1939–40 directory. Skidmore had served as chief of design at the 1933 Century of Progress Exposition. His brother-in-law, Nathaniel Owings, was chief of construction. In 1936, when the firm moved into the Monroe, it was designing homes in a Highland Park subdivision. Two years later, it was hired to modernize the Monadnock Building. Graham Aldis, Owen Aldis's nephew and the president of the Building Managers' Association, announced the project with much fanfare. "We believe our demonstration of progressive styling in the Monadnock building will offer a solution to other property owners that will be widely adopted, that is, rebuilding within the existing walls rather than adding to the demolition of millions of dollars worth of Loop skyscrapers," he said. The firm was the perfect choice, Skidmore and Owings having performed magic at the world's fair.

Other prominent firms filled the offices downstairs. By 1912, Owen Aldis had figured out how to subdivide skyscraper offices in a manner that produced the most rent and provided the most light. In the late nineteenth century, when the first skyscrapers were built, electric lighting was in its infancy, and tenants relied on natural light. Interior offices surrounded light courts, and those that faced the street had expansive Chicago windows to bring in as much daylight as possible.

Because electric light was so much brighter by 1912, the windows in the Monroe Building could be slightly smaller than traditional Chicago windows. These narrow double-hung windows made it possible to build more interior walls and subdivide into small rooms. Offices became office suites. The interior space, which connected to windowed offices, served as reception or waiting rooms, stenographers' offices, or filing areas. Once again, here the skyscraper was perfected.

Holabird & Roche took the entire fourteenth floor of the Monroe Building. Holabird took a corner office; Roche was next to him. Then, along the power row, came the firm's third partner, Edward Renwick, followed by the business manager and general superintendent. Architects, draftsmen, and stenographers filled out the floor.

The firm of Schmidt, Garden & Martin (later Schmidt, Garden & Erikson), which designed the Montgomery Ward Warehouse on the Chicago River and the Ambassador Hotel on the Near North Side, had its offices on the eleventh floor of the Monroe Building for decades. And Howard Van Doren Shaw rented space for his firm on the fifteenth floor until his death in 1926. Shaw was noted for his graceful designs of country homes in Lake Forest and for the village's Market Square, one of America's first shopping centers.

With architects came blueprint companies, renderers, paint pigment specialists, and, of course, engineers. Corydon T. Purdy, who in 1889 devised the structural system for the first skyscraper framed all in steel, the Rand McNally Building, maintained an office on the fifteenth floor. By 1911, the Rand McNally Building was torn down to make way for a taller building. Corydon Purdy's firm, Purdy & Henderson, worked with Holabird & Roche for decades. Joseph Strauss, whose Strauss Bascule Bridge Company built bridges around the world, worked out of the sixth floor. "Building a bridge is a war with the forces of nature," said Strauss, who would go on to construct the Golden Gate Bridge.

HOLABIRD & ROCHE
ARCHITECTS
RANDOLPH 5960 1400 MONROE BLDG.
104 S. MICHIGAN AVENUE

WALTER BURLEY GRIFFIN
FRANCIS BARRY BYRNE
ARCHITECTS · LANDSCAPE ARCHITECT
1600 MONROE BUILDING
104 SOUTH MICHIGAN AVENUE CHICAGO ILLINOIS TELEPHONE RANDOLPH 3268

IANNELLI STUDIOS
1601 MONROE BLDG. CHICAGO
A. IANNELLI
M. IANNELLI

COMPANY LETTERHEADS OF EARLY MONROE BUILDING TENANTS.

**ALTHOUGH ARCHITECTS TOOK THE UPPER FLOORS** of the Monroe Building, the majority of tenants during its first several decades were physicians. Isaac Abt, a pediatrician who preferred to be called simply a "baby doctor," founded what would become the Infant Welfare Society of Chicago. John J. Killeen, an eye, ear, nose, and throat specialist, was the medical adviser to the Chicago Civic Opera Company, and Philip H. Kreuscher was an orthopedic surgeon who helped major-league ballplayers recover from injuries. His operation to replace torn ligaments in Hall of Famer Dixie Walker's throwing arm in 1937 was hailed as "one of the greatest pieces of baseball surgery."

The Monroe's most prominent physician was John B. Murphy, an abdominal surgeon called "the surgical genius of our generation" by no less than William Mayo. None of Murphy's colleagues doubted his ability and knowledge, but they did question his penchant for grabbing headlines. Murphy, whose office was on the eighth floor, first gained fame in 1886 when he stayed up all night to treat the wounds of thirty policemen involved in the Haymarket riot. In 1912, he ordered that a special train rush Theodore Roosevelt from Milwaukee to Chicago after the former president was shot during his campaign against President William Howard Taft. "It takes more than one bullet to kill a Bull Moose," Roosevelt famously said. Roosevelt spent

A LARGE MONROE BUILDING OFFICE. TENANTS DEPENDED ON THE BUILDING'S LARGE WINDOWS TO BATHE OFFICE SPACE IN LIGHT.

four days under Murphy's care at Chicago's Mercy Hospital. The shooting derailed his campaign to win back the presidency.

**THE MONROE WAS THE LAST MAJOR BUILDING DEVELOPED** by Peter and Shepherd Brooks. Peter Brooks died in 1920, and his brother died two years later. Their eighty-two-acre summer retreat in Massachusetts is now owned by the City of Medford and is open to the public. Holabird and Roche kept working. Their firm built hundreds of buildings after the Monroe Building, including Soldier Field. Holabird died in 1923; Roche died in 1927. The firm was renamed Holabird & Root after Holabird's son, John Augur Holabird, and John Root's son, John Wellborn Root Jr., took control.

The year 1912 was the start of a new life for Aldis. His wife had passed away in 1885, and his only son died of measles in 1903. By the turn of the century, Aldis was a world traveler. He met nineteen-year-old Marie Madeleine Dumas on a motoring trip through Europe. She took care of him following a car accident in which he broke his arm. She knew no English; he knew no French. The *Chicago Tribune* described the relationship in a front-page headline:

Owen Aldis in Motor Romance
Will Wed Count's Daughter.

Chicago Widower of 60 Intends to Marry
French Girl Third His Age Who Cared
For Him When He was Hurt

The couple was married in November 1912 in Paris, lived there and in Chicago, and traveled the world. He died in 1925; she died in 1981.

Rookwood shut down its architectural department in the 1930s. Tastes changed, and there was less demand for architectural ornament, particularly for interior ceramics. The Northwestern Terra Cotta Company closed in 1965.

**BY 1913, MICHIGAN AVENUE HAD A NEW FEEL,** according to Martyn Johnson, an actor who later became the publisher of *The Dial,* a prominent national magazine based in Chicago. He returned to Chicago that year from a long trip to Europe and found that a remarkable change had taken place in the city's appearance and spirit. "As I emerged from the Twelfth street station I was eager to see what Chicago would be like after the old world," he wrote. "But I was not prepared for what I saw. As I gazed down that wonderful perspective of Michigan Avenue my emotion was one of mingled exhilaration and awe. It is the most beautiful street I ever have seen. Chicago has made it. It is Chicago. In that monumental row of buildings is the index of Chicago's character."

Not everyone, of course, agreed. In 1912, Manierre Dawson, a progressive artist who worked as a draftsman for Holabird & Roche, wrote in his journal about "the ridiculous Monroe building, who wants a medieval Italian building on Michigan Avenue." One man told the *Tribune* in 1913 that he'd complained to police about the loud echoes that cars made as they roared down Monroe Street between the University Club and Monroe Building. "The reverberation between the buildings is almost deafening," he said. "Not only was nothing done, but I did not have the courtesy of a reply."

Frank Lloyd Wright was more biting. In 1918, at the Art Institute of Chicago, he declared: "A Chicago smokestack has more quality as a work of art than the effete gray ghosts of a dubious past at the foot of Monroe Street."

Wright was taking aim at the University Club and the Monroe Building (which he would nonetheless move his offices into the following year). He also called Holabird & Roche's 1911 City Hall and County Building "a big bluff in vain classic costing thousands a month for great columns that are a huge and expensive load to carry instead of carrying the load."

And he didn't stop there. He aimed right at the beloved homes of Chicago's elite, questioning their conventional tastes. "See the assortment of homes on the drive or any favored section of the city. See our rich in their evening clothes at the opera, our badly overdressed business women in their tall white shoes or their equivalent on the street," he said. "We are plundering the old world of all its finery and dressing ourselves in it as a kind

HOLABIRD & ROCHE MOVED ITS OFFICES TO THE MONROE BUILDING IN 1912 AND STAYED UNTIL 1928.

of masquerade. This is not culture in any real sense."

Despite Wright's words, the Monroe Building persevered. Its changing tenants over the next century hint at the changes that were taking place all over the world. During World War I, Chicagoans rallied around the building because it was the Chicago headquarters of the American Red Cross. In 1918, a temporary monument with the names of all the soldiers and sailors who had died in the Great War was installed in Grant Park directly across from the Monroe.

During the late 1910s, as cars started dominating the streets of Chicago, the building became the home of several automotive businesses. The Boulevard Tire & Supply Store took an office on the seventh floor; Hardman Tire & Rubber and the Chicago Standard Axle Company moved into the third floor. At the height of the Depression, personnel agencies rented space, and during the 1940s, war-related groups like the Military Order of the Purple Heart became tenants. In 1944, Northwest Airlines took over the first-floor corner space that had been occupied by Capper & Capper. Northwest's president explained that he expected a huge influx of passengers after the war.

The Monroe was home to several foreign consulates after World War II. In 1978, two terrorists invaded the West German Consulate on the tenth floor and held six people hostage, demanding the release of a Croatian

THE STYLES AND LAYOUT OF OFFICES AND OFFICE FRONTS HAVE CHANGED DRAMATICALLY THROUGHOUT THE BUILDING.

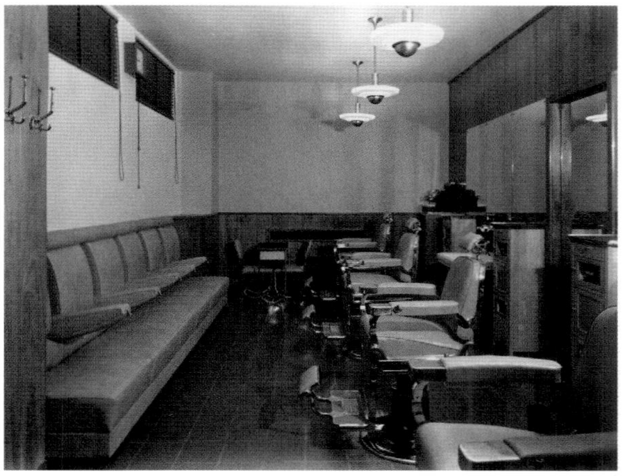

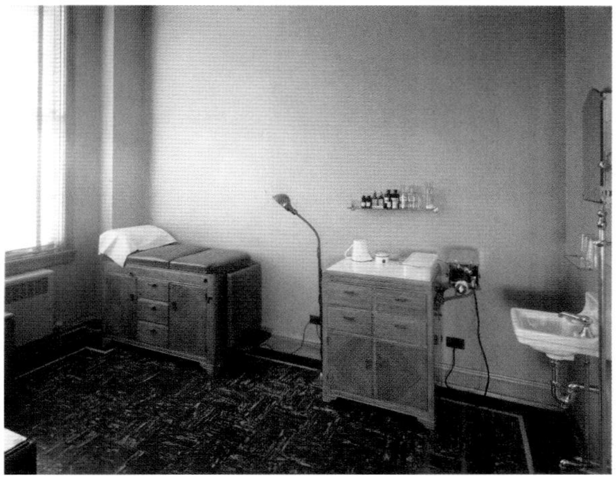

THE MONROE BUILDING NEAR THE CENTER OF THE MICHIGAN AVENUE STREETWALL AROUND 1957. PRESERVING THE HISTORIC MICHIGAN BOULEVARD DISTRICT IS A MAJOR REASON WHY THE BUILDING WAS PURCHASED AND RESTORED. THE TWELVE-BLOCK DISTRICT WAS DESIGNATED AS A CHICAGO LANDMARK IN 2002.

GARLAND BUILDING
JOHN M. SMYTH CO.

**AN UPPER-FLOOR ELEVATOR LOBBY. THE MONROE BUILDING WAS MODERNIZED MANY TIMES DURING ITS FIRST HUNDRED YEARS.**

nationalist from a West German jail. In 1989, two thousand students demonstrated outside the Chinese Consulate there, protesting the Tiananmen Square massacre. A year later, another group of demonstrators marched outside the Salvadoran Consulate in the Monroe Building, calling for an end of U.S. aid to El Salvador.

The Monroe kept a high profile on the street but not in the history of Chicago architecture. Although the building was conceived and designed by the advance guard of modern architecture, the influential critics of the Chicago School never took it seriously.

Lewis Mumford, one of the nation's first urban scholars, wrote about Chicago and architecture. His *Sticks and Stones: A Study of American Architecture and*

*Civilization* (1924) was one of the earliest attempts at a full-blown history of American architecture, and he focused on Chicago. "Like so many intellectuals of the period, he was obsessed with what was and what wasn't peculiarly American about American architecture," said Robert Bruegmann, the Holabird & Roche authority. "Because of this interest, he focused on H. H. Richardson since Richardson seemed to be charting a new path that was not heavily dependent on European precedent."

Mumford was primarily interested in the Loop's skyscrapers and the city's Prairie School residences. "I have never gone looking to see if there is any indication that he knew the Monroe Building, and I don't know what he would have made of it if he had stopped to consider it," Bruegmann wrote. "I suspect it would have been somewhat ambivalent. He might have said that the gable roof and ornament was incongruous on a tall office building, but it is quite possible he would have admired the skill with which they were deployed."

In the mid-twentieth century, Carl Condit, the essential local historian of the Chicago School, wrote four books about Chicago architecture. He mentioned hundreds of buildings, but he never mentioned the Monroe. Unlike The Rookery and the Monadnock, Marquette, and Reliance Buildings, the Monroe was forgotten.

For decades, the building fell victim to a series of remodeling regimes that shrouded its beauty. Owners tried to keep up with the times; they installed new switchboards, automated the elevators, sealed the windows from the eleventh to fourteenth floors for central air-conditioning, and added polished brass panels on the two entrances. Upstairs, they installed marble over the Rookwood wall tiles, carpeted over the Rookwood floors, and suspended fluorescent lights and acoustical tile from office and corridor ceilings. The building was pushed and pulled and retrofitted to appear modern so that it could attract tenants. The original entrances on Michigan Avenue and Monroe Street were reworked, the custom Rookwood tile floor in the lobby was replaced by a standard terrazzo, the wood molding was trashed, and the leaking skylights were covered with tar paper.

By the turn of the twenty-first century, the Monroe Building was waiting to be rediscovered.

# Restoration

"We see ourselves as preservationists first and developers second."

Sean McGowan, chief operating officer of Tawani Enterprises

WORKING BENEATH THE PROJECTING EAVES ABOARD THE MAST CLIMBER.

**IT TOOK SIX YEARS TO RESTORE AND REHABILITATE** the Monroe Building—five years longer than it took to build it. The object was to transform the century-old building into a twenty-first-century new age skyscraper while incorporating as many historic details as possible.

The process seemed daunting at first. The Monroe had undergone decades of disastrous rehabilitation. Its graceful front and side doors had long been junked. Its ceramic lobby was damaged, and its classic elevator system had been covered over. Carpeting blanketed tile floors. Windows and transoms were walled up. The Spanish tiles on the roof were cracked, the building's terra-cotta skin was camouflaged by soot and smoke, and its windows appeared battered, many modified or replaced for air-conditioning systems.

"When I first walked in the building, I didn't quite get what it could be," said Michael Voorheis, an architect who worked on the Monroe. "It was torn apart, dingy. But I remember the first time we came out and they removed the scaffolding. It was clean; all the windows were complete. This is when I realized it was a pretty remarkable building."

Jennifer Pritzker, who restored and redeveloped the Monroe, saw the building's potential. She bought it to house the Pritzker Military Museum & Library. But she also bought it to make a statement about the value of Chicago's grand old skyscrapers. She regarded the Monroe as a crucial part of Chicago's historic Michigan Avenue Streetwall and a long-lost element of the eastern entrance to the Loop.

Architects and builders had to figure out the best way to update the building while keeping it substantially original. Plumbing and electrical systems were replaced, central air-conditioning for the entire building was installed, a new heating plant was built, security was upgraded, and a data center with an on-site server was set up. Added to the building were a fitness center, an area for bike storage, a conference center, and a three-story auditorium.

Tawani Enterprises, Jennifer Pritzker's management company, essentially built an entirely new structure inside the Monroe Building. Its obsolete light court was replaced by fifteen new levels housing mechanical equipment, heating and air-conditioning systems, stairwells, and restrooms. By filling the space with what architect Thomas Lassin called "a building within a building," the architects transformed the horseshoe-shaped Monroe, which had been built around the forty-by-fifty-foot court, into a standard rectangular modern skyscraper, markedly increasing the building's rentable space and making technological and structural changes possible.

"It was part restoration and part renovation," said Lassin, project manager for Holabird & Root. "We tried to find original fabric and bring the building up to modern building codes and real estate standards."

To fully understand the building, architects used a nearly complete set of construction documents. Holabird & Root, the successor firm of Holabird & Roche, donated the company's blueprints and building documents to the

MONROE BUILDING BROCHURE FROM THE 1950S. IT BOASTS: "YOUR CUSTOMERS, EXECUTIVES, AND EMPLOYES WILL FIND YOUR NEW OFFICE QUARTERS IN THE MONROE BUILDING EASY TO REACH FROM ANY PART OF THE CITY."

Chicago Historical Society around 1980, and the firm was able to consult those records. Architects and builders found many of the original elements—doors, doorknobs, transoms, and elevators—stashed in the attic or basement or buried beneath the many remodelings.

Pritzker's vision of a modern building steeped in historical authenticity was clear from the start, said Dave Linden, vice president of Bulley & Andrews, which was the general contractor for the renovation. "I would call it a gut rehab, but we tried to salvage, reuse, or replicate as many historic components as possible," he explained. "What made it very unusual was the owner's commitment to the restoration process. You don't see that too often."

**THE BROOKS FAMILY RETAINED OWNERSHIP** of the Monroe Building until 1968. The property then changed hands several times before it was bought in 1978 by a limited partnership headed by Charles L. Strobeck. During those years, the building was managed by Strobeck Reiss & Company (later Strobeck Real Estate), which had acquired Aldis & Company, the property management company founded by Owen Aldis and his brother, Arthur.

In 2005, Winthrop Properties purchased the Monroe for about $22 million. The firm bought the building for its potential: it was in a prime location, overlooking Millennium Park and the Art Institute of Chicago, a stretch that was fast becoming the city's cultural and recreational mecca.

Bob Horner, a partner at Winthrop, saw the office building as a residential tower. He planned to gut the Monroe to build condominiums.

WINTHROP PROPERTIES BROCHURE ADVERTISES NINETY-SIX EXCLUSIVE RESIDENCES FOR SALE IN 2005. "THE MONROE SPOKE OF GRACE, AFFLUENCE, SUCCESS. TODAY, THE GOLDEN AGE LIVES AGAIN IN THE BOULEVARD."

"Like other older office buildings, this building has floor plates that are too small for today's major class A tenants," he told the *Chicago Tribune.* "In today's environment large tenants don't like to be spread across many floors."

Winthrop's proposal to convert the building into ninety-six residential condominiums was approved by the Chicago Plan Commission. The second through fourteenth floors would be one-, two-, and three-bedroom condos. The fifteenth and sixteenth floors would be two-, four-, and six-bedroom units that could be customized or combined. The Monroe, to be renamed the Boulevard, would also offer parking on its lower floors.

"We were attracted to just about everything in the building," said Horner. "We liked the architecture, the unique tile work in the lobby, and the fact that it was created by a woman-owned company, the layout of the units, and the views from almost every direction." The restored building would give residents unobstructed views of Lake Michigan to the east, the University Club to the north, and the Sears Tower to the west. "We were also fascinated by the height of the ceilings and the sturdiness of the building," Horner added.

Work was progressing quickly in 2005. The firm hired FitzGerald Associates Architects to draw up plans and opened model apartments on the second floor. Within weeks, reservations were placed for almost half of the residential units. Then Horner received a call from a broker asking if his firm would be interested in selling.

"While we are never wedded to any building, this one was pretty well along," he said. Horner doubted that anybody could make an offer high enough to offset the money that had already been spent on the building. The price, he said, would have to reflect the effort that had gone into the building and the potential for profit.

The offer was from J&J Arnaco, Jennifer Pritzker's real estate holding company. As mentioned, Pritzker was interested in purchasing the Monroe Building because she wanted a home for the Pritzker Military Museum & Library, which opened in 2003 at 610 North Fairbanks Court as the Pritzker Military Library. The research library was created to foster a broader understanding of American military history and the role of citizen-soldiers, men and women who train for military duty and are ready to serve in times of emergency, primarily in the National Guard and Army Reserve. Pritzker served in the U.S. Army, the Army Reserve, and the Illinois National Guard for twenty-seven years. She retired in 2001 and was promoted to the honorary rank of colonel in the Illinois Army National Guard.

Afterward, Pritzker spent millions on Chicago real estate—money to purchase, rehab, or restore the Emil Bach House, a Prairie School residence designed by Frank Lloyd Wright, the Morse Theater, and several apartment buildings on Chicago's North Side and in the northern suburbs.

Pritzker was looking for a vintage freestanding building downtown with a beautiful lobby that could house her military library. She wanted the library on the second floor so that it would be easily accessible by way of stairs or elevator.

But she also saw her move as part of a rescue mission. She opposed the idea of turning the Monroe into a condominium building and wanted to preserve as much of the Historic Michigan Boulevard District as possible. As Pritzker told the *Chicago Tribune* in 2011, she hoped that the Monroe would serve as "a model of an architectural restoration that successfully preserves historic character while providing an excellent home for its tenants."

Pritzker offered Winthrop $31.2 million, a figure that Horner called "a fair and generous offer." Horner's architect, Patrick FitzGerald, was startled when he was told to stop final plans for the building. "The developer knew that he had a hit on his hands, and I couldn't figure out how anybody could purchase the building and make it work," he said. But FitzGerald ended up being pleased: "As a fan of architecture, I'm glad we didn't convert it."

**PRITZKER AND HER TEAM CHOSE** to use many of the building's original contractors for the restoration. She hired Holabird & Root to do architectural and engineering work, Ludowici Roof Tile to manufacture replacement roof tiles, and the Rookwood Pottery Company to restore its tile work.

The first order of business was a critical inspection of all four sides of the building, focusing on the terra-cotta cladding on the Michigan Avenue and Monroe Street facades. It took about two years for workers to check and fix the damaged terra cotta, which had withstood nearly a century of Chicago weather, to clean the exterior with chemicals, to grind the joints, to tuck-point

TERRA-COTTA ORNAMENT FOUND BEHIND THE BASEMENT BOILER. THE PIECE LED ARCHITECTS TO UNDERSTAND HOW THE TWO CORNICES TERMINATED.

the building using mortar that matched the original, and to replace or restore the windows.

Terra cotta should last for centuries, but the steel that attaches it to the framework of a building can rust if water gets underneath it. Inspectors look for rust stains and signs of swelling steel. They tap and listen to the terra cotta to detect problems. With most buildings, they ride on a swing-stage scaffold (the kind that window washers use) for hands-on inspection, but another system was needed to get up close to the Monroe.

"The primary challenge for the restoration was access to the facades," said Mary Brush, the architect who was in charge of the inspection. "The steeply pitched roof and terra-cotta cornice precluded the option for swing-stage access." So contractors built a device known as a mast climber, a scaffold with a motorized work platform that scales a building vertically. Mast climbers are generally anchored to the structural steel of a building. Brush and Chris Lee of Bulley & Andrews Masonry Restoration rejected that idea because of the damage it might cause the terra cotta; instead, workers tied the mast climber to the interior structure through windows on the thirteenth floor.

Although the Monroe's gable roof and cornice made inspecting the

"WE LEARNED A LOT ABOUT EARLY TWENTIETH-CENTURY CONSTRUCTION WHEN WE GUTTED THIS BUILDING," SAID CONTRACTOR MIKE LEMMONS.

EVERY EXTERIOR WINDOW WAS REMOVED DURING RESTORATION. GLASS WAS CLEANED AND FIXED WHEN NECESSARY, BUT PANES WERE NOT REPLACED.

SOME INTERIOR OFFICE WINDOWS WERE RESTORED. NEW TENANTS WITH FULL FLOORS OFTEN PREFER REMOVING THE GLASS TO OPEN THEIR SPACE.

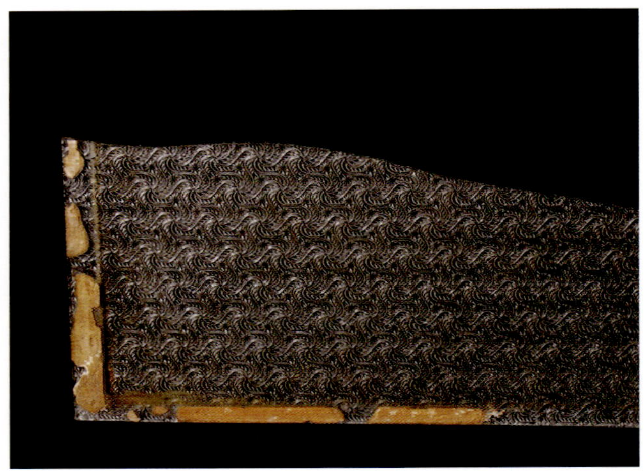

TO REPLICATE THE FEEL OF ORIGINAL GLASS, THE MONROE'S OWNER SOUGHT OUT A COMPANY TO CREATE PATTERNS THAT REFLECT WINDOWS OF THE ERA.

BRONZE ENTRANCE PANELS AND REVOLVING DOORS FROM THE 1950S WERE REMOVED AND REPLACED WITH SWING DOORS FOR THE BUILDING'S TWO ENTRANCES.

THE CAST-IRON FANTAIL ABOVE THE ENTRANCE DOORS IS ASSEMBLED IN A KANSAS FOUNDRY. ILLINOIS BRONZE WORKS SUPERVISED ALL METALWORK.

THE CHIMERA—A MONSTER THAT WAS PART LION, PART SNAKE AND PART GOAT FROM GREEK MYTHOLOGY—TERMINATES THE BUILDING'S TWO CORNICES.

REMOVED FROM THE BUILDING LONG AGO, THE FOUR CHIMERAS WERE RECAST IN TERRA COTTA AND INSTALLED ONCE AGAIN IN THE PEDIMENT.

MOST OF THE BUILDING'S EIGHT SKYLIGHTS WERE COVERED OVER WHEN RESTORATION STARTED. THEY WERE REPLACED WITH HIGH-TECH GLASS.

THE VIEW ACROSS MONROE STREET OF THE UNIVERSITY CLUB. ARCHITECTS USED TO DRAW BENEATH THE SKYLIGHTS. NOW A MARKETING FIRM FILLS THE SPACE.

COPPER FLASHING IS INSTALLED ALONG WITH A HORIZONTAL AND VERTICAL BATTEN SYSTEM THAT WILL HOLD THE SPANISH-STYLE TILES.

"YOU REALLY CAN'T SEE HOW BEAUTIFUL THE ROOF IS FROM THE GROUND," SAID TAB COLBERT OF LUDOWICI ROOF TILE.

building difficult, the broad overhang had protected the front facade from rain for a century, keeping water away and most of the steel attachments dry. "We were amazed to see what great condition the metal was in," said Lee. It looked almost new—and, after a cleaning, so did the terra cotta.

"The terra cotta was in remarkably good condition for its age and perpetual weather damage from an eastward exposure to Grant Park and Lake Michigan," Brush later wrote. "Building cleaning revealed a subtle striping pattern in the terra cotta that had been obtained by varying the proportions of speckle glaze." The building, with its newly visible horizontal bands of pinkish beige and brown, seems to change color depending on the light. Along Monroe Street, the terra cotta takes on a cold grayish cast in the indirect sunlight. But with the sun from the east, the Michigan Avenue facade acquires a vibrant salmon appearance.

A cantilevered platform was built on the fourteenth floor to provide access to the upper floors, cornice, and roof. Brush checked every piece of terra cotta. About 370 of them—roughly 4 percent of the facade—were damaged and needed to be replaced. Because the pieces could be removed, remaking them was not a problem. But the cornice's end pieces were a mystery. They were missing, and no drawings showed exactly how the cornice terminated.

"There's an ongoing joke in the restoration business that somebody will always find something behind the basement boiler," Brush said. "And that's just what happened. We found broken pieces of terra cotta, black and sooty, that had come from the ends of the cornices. When you put them side by side, they turned out to be the head of a lion, the head of a goat, and the tail of a snake. We knew the cornice motif was primarily an undulating grapevine, but we couldn't figure out how these animals fit."

Then Brush remembered the Chimera, a creature in Greek mythology that was a mix of a lion, a goat, and a snake. The Chimera and other damaged pieces were sent to Lincoln, California, where they were refabricated by Gladding, McBean, one of only two major terra-cotta manufacturers still in business. Matching the physical dimension of the terra cotta was straightforward; matching the unique glazing was not.

Most of the windows were restored rather than replaced. The wood sashes—old-growth oak with mahogany trim—on the Michigan Avenue and Monroe Street facades were stripped and refinished, and Restoration Works, based in Bradley, Illinois, replaced the rotted wood. Microscopic analysis determined that the original color of the sashes was a very dark green. "Returning to that color had a great effect," said Mary Brush. "The windows just fell back and made the subtle striping color come out."

The metal sash windows on the alley facing west were also stripped and reputtied. Some of the polished wire glass was replaced, but most was cleaned.

"A decision was made to keep the single-pane windows [on the Michigan and Monroe facades]," said Dave Linden. "It was not the most energy-efficient decision, but it was made for historical reasons." Double-paned windows would be slightly tinted and give the building a different

A RESTORED DORMER AND SKYLIGHT ON THE ROOF. PHOTO BY MARK BALLOGG.

profile. "Replacing the windows and adding a pane would have been less expensive but would have been inaccurate," said Peder Dahlberg, who oversaw the Monroe's restoration. "Glass was integral. It took up 50 percent of the exterior wall."

**AFTER THE BUILDING'S TERRA COTTA** and windows were restored, workers turned their attention to the roof. The deep green Spanish tiles were stamped by the Ludowici-Celadon Company, which had been headquartered in the Monroe Building for decades. "We looked up to see if the company was still in business," said Dahlberg. "They were, and they still had the molds."

But as with the re-creation of the terra cotta, making new roof tiles that matched the originals proved to be a challenge. Tab Colbert, CEO of the company now known as Ludowici Roof Tile and based in New Lexington, Ohio, said the original clay tiles had been manufactured in kilns that were less predictable and exact than those today. The color of a tile had depended on where it was placed in the kiln. Every batch was inconsistent, and each tile had a slightly different coloration.

The company sent a batch of perfectly colored new tiles, but Pritzker's team wanted the roof to appear as historically accurate as possible. "They wanted a slight imperfection, which would make the building look more original and handmade," Colbert said.

"When we got our first tests, the shape of the tiles was perfect, but the color was not," said Dahlberg. "They made a range of greens, but none of it looked quite right."

The process had changed, making it harder to reproduce the tiles. "The original tiles had a sort of beautiful iridescence to them," said Lassin. "In those days, heavy metals were used to make that look, and it is no longer able to use them in ceramics."

Eventually, Ludowici's color chemists figured out how to fool the eye. The replacement tiles blended various greens with a custom speckle to give the appearance of a natural variation of color, said Mary Brush. Ludowici produced tiles with slightly different colors—a dark glaze with light speckles and a light glaze with dark speckles. When mixed together on the roof, the multicolored tiles somehow appeared to replicate the original color.

Another century-old company, Knickerbocker Roofing & Paving of Harvey, Illinois, removed the old tile, installed a new substructure and roofing battens, experimented with a new fastening system, and laid the new tiles. They also built extensive copper gutters, roof valleys, and flashing around the building's eight skylights and three dormers. They worked through the winter of 2009 and into the spring of 2010. "We did roofing during the day and hoisting during the night," said Chris Cronin, Knickerbocker's president.

Because the roof had been changed dramatically over the years, it needed to be modified to return it to its original design. The original drawings showed seven small skylights, but over the years most had been covered up to prevent leaking.

"We were going through the drawings one day when we found this little sheet, not even a full sheet, kind of tucked in the drawings," recalled Dahlberg. "It was a section showing a skylight on the sixteenth floor."

The sheet was dated 1912, a year after the original drawings and the year the Monroe opened. But neither the twelve-by-seventy-two-foot skylight nor the structure that supported existed.

"Looking at the building, we couldn't see any evidence it was really there," said Dahlberg. "We didn't know if they drew it up for a tenant and didn't put it in or what, so we went to the Chicago History Museum and asked

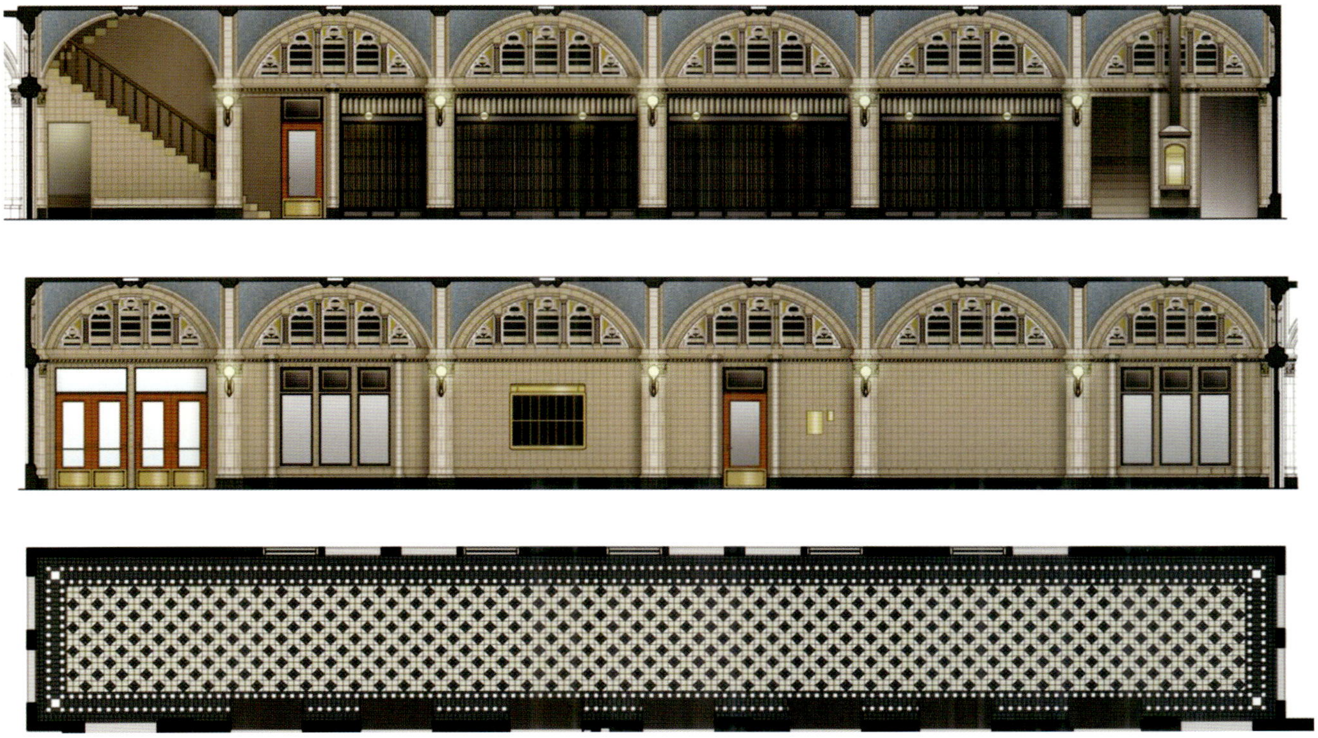

if they had any aerial photos of Chicago. We found two photos taken by the Illinois National Guard in 1936 flying across the lakefront. There we saw it. The skylight had been put in, but by 1936 it had already been tarred over. You could still see it was there because the structure was still there. That was a big surprise."

The restoration team decided that it should be rebuilt. But opening up the roof for the huge skylight was particularly formidable because tenants still maintained offices in the building. Workers needed to keep the building weatherproof while it was open to the elements. They devised a crude tarp system to protect the exposed top floor from rain and snow. Explained Mike Lemmons, senior project manager at Bulley & Andrews: "We let the water come in through the tarps and then directed it out of the building. Some days were hairy, living in Chicago."

HOLABIRD & ROOT'S PLANS FOR THE RESTORED LOBBY. THE TOP SKETCH SHOWS THE ELEVATORS ON THE NORTH SIDE OF THE LOBBY. THE MIDDLE SKETCH SHOWS THE OPPOSITE WALL. THE BOTTOM SKETCH SHOWS THE TILE PATTERN OF THE ROOKWOOD FLOOR.

**WORK INSIDE WAS LESS FRAUGHT** with weather problems, but bringing the interior back to 1912 was just as demanding.

Building records were clear that Rookwood had manufactured the distinctive lobby tiles, but the Cincinnati company was barely in business by the early twenty-first century. It had survived bankruptcy and reorganization but was teetering once again, with fewer than thirty employees, when Pritzker's team called to see if it could re-create the tiles in the lobby.

In the 1950s, the Brooks family installed a terrazzo floor in the lobby. "In their defense, the tile was pretty worn out," said Dahlberg. "And it needed to be replaced. Terrazzo was much cheaper and much quicker to install."

Early photographs showed the pattern of the lobby floor, and records hinted at the color. An original floor was found beneath the carpeting in an upper-level elevator lobby. Once again, the challenge was to produce a glazed tile that looked vintage, weathered, slightly inconsistent, and handcrafted.

"Since we had to mimic age progression to match hundred-year-old tiles, this project took extensive research and testing," said Jim Robinson, a glaze chemist at Rookwood. "We used an extraordinarily wear-resistant floor tile glaze and sophisticated color variation to create a visually resonant installation."

More exacting than creating the lobby floor anew was producing about two hundred tiles to replace those that were broken or damaged. "It was mind-boggling," said Robinson. "We had to make pieces that would shrink to the original size and match century-old pieces already on the wall." Rookwood artists had to replicate the coloration and create crackled patterns, known as crazing, which were enhanced by staining the tiles with India ink. They were successful: "Even under close inspection, it will be virtually impossible to detect the new tiles from those made in 1911," said Robinson.

It would have been easier to just replace all the tiles, but in the interest of historical authenticity, Dahlberg wanted to retain as many as possible. "The biggest challenge was getting the Rookwood tile to look right," he said. "That's the building's signature. It's the first thing you see when you walk inside."

"We all learned just how brilliant and inventive the original Rookwood designers were," said Robinson. "They produced high-fired glazes that were extraordinarily beautiful."

Once the new lobby tiles were approved, the next task was installing them with what Robinson called "beautiful irregularity." Said Mike Lemmons: "They asked us to install the tiles as it would have been installed one hundred years ago. Nowadays, we use spacers. We would install the tile precisely. They did it by hand, so we had to make it look handmade."

The Monroe Building job saved Rookwood but almost killed it, Robinson admitted. The company returned to the faience business, creating architectural ceramics, but its work on the Monroe tested its capacity during the economic downturn. "This was our first monumental job in our new plant," he said. "It took us two years, and put a strain on us, but we made it through."

**THE TWO ENTRANCES TO THE MONROE BUILDING**—one on Michigan Avenue and one on Monroe Street—had been changed dramatically over the years. Revolving doors replaced the two sets of swing doors at both entrances in the 1920s. Bronze panels were installed in the 1950s to make the building look more modern. Gone were the cast-iron doorframes and transoms. And gone was the distinctive fanlight, an arched glass panel graced by ornamental steel filigree, above each entrance.

Photos and construction documents of the original entrances showed the profile of the doors, but it was unclear what the original fanlights looked like. Designers in the early 1900s often modeled ornament on existing work,

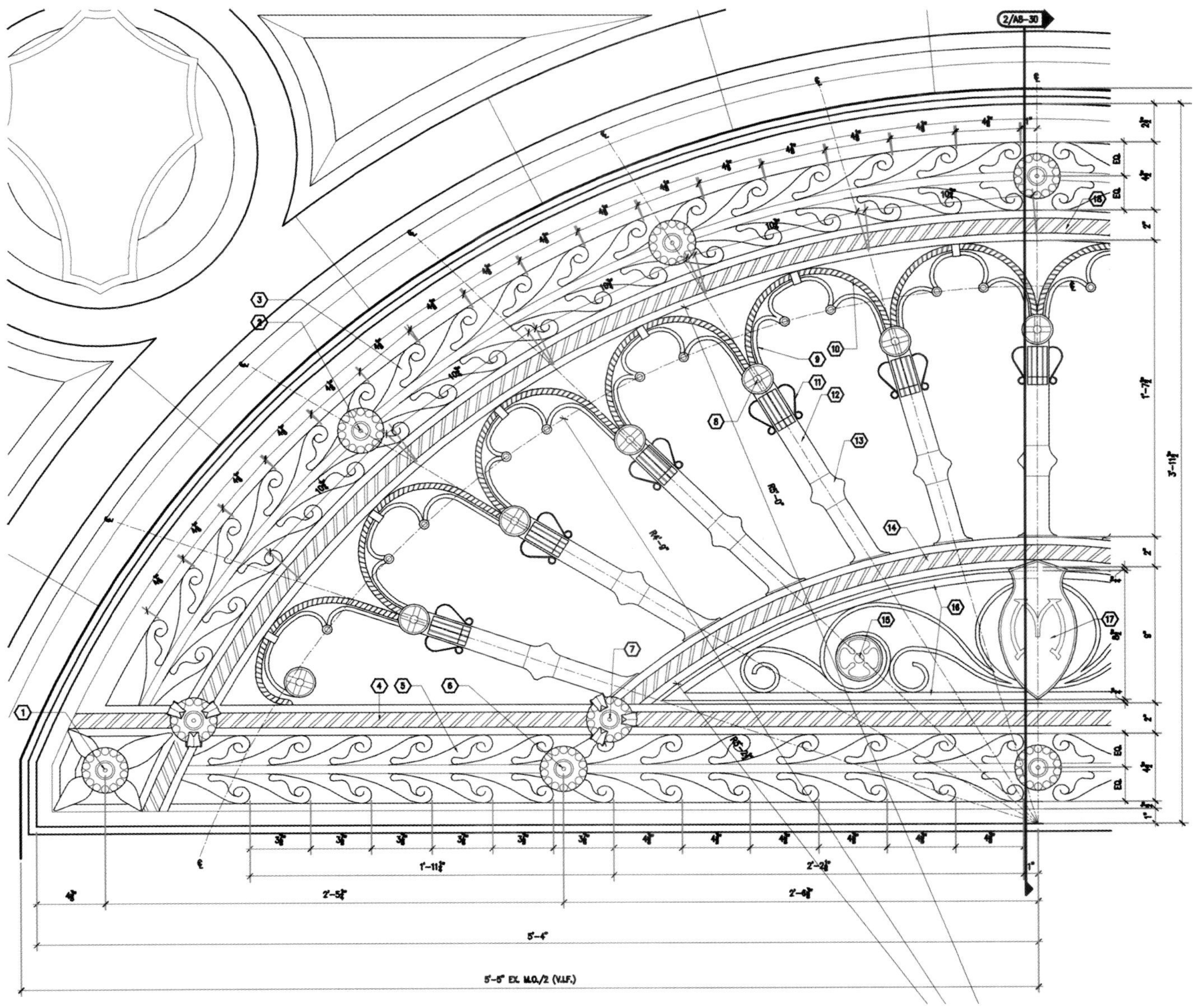

and the architects at Holabird & Roche were no exception. They paged through the firm's old reference books on decorative ironwork, and there, on page 49 of *Wrought Iron in Architecture* by Gerald K. Geerlings, was a photograph of the arched grille over the main entrance of the sixteenth-century Monastero Delle Barbantine, the town hall of Lucca, Italy. It was clearly the inspiration for the Monroe's fanlights.

The new fanlights were fabricated by Janet Zoble and Tim Degginger of Deggingers' Foundry in Topeka, Kansas. Zoble generated computer drawings and three-dimensional renderings of the fanlights and then sculpted the decorative elements. Individual components were then cast in iron and attached to a stainless steel frame. The fanlights were assembled in the foundry to be certain the pieces fit, then disassembled and shipped to Chicago for reassembly.

The Topeka foundry also re-created the cast-iron vestibule door

COMPUTER-GENERATED DRAWING OF THE FANLIGHT'S COMPONENT PARTS THAT WERE RE-CREATED TO SIT ABOVE THE TWO SETS OF ENTRY DOORS.

frames. The originals had been removed when the revolving doors were put in, but with the exterior swing doors reinstalled, the vestibule doors were needed again to stabilize air pressure in the lobby.

Deggingers' was hired by MTH Industries and Illinois Bronze Works, which was in charge of the metalwork in the building's lobby and upper floors. Illinois Bronze's Lou Nutini directed the lobby restoration; coincidentally, his father, Anthony Nutini, had supervised the 1956 Monroe remodeling. "We removed all of the bronze that he had built," Lou Nutini said, "and re-created what he had taken out."

BRONZE SCONCES WERE MANUFACTURED FOR THE MAIN LOBBY TO MATCH THE ORIGINALS SEEN IN ARCHIVAL PHOTOGRAPHS.

Nutini's major job was remodeling the elevator shafts. The shafts were originally open, but building codes now prohibited that. Peder Dahlberg had assumed that the elevator grilles were scrapped decades ago. But riding up a shaft on the roof of an elevator cab one day, he found them hidden behind the marble walls that had been added in a remodeling. They were removed, sent to Illinois Bronze to be stripped and painted their original color, and reinstalled.

Six new elevator cabs were built to look like their predecessors but with up-to-date electronics. Workers at Globe Architectural and Metal in Germantown, Wisconsin, spent more than five hundred hours manufacturing each cab. "We used quartered white oak, bronze handrails, aluminum grilles, and brass inserts to turn back the clock," said Al Koenig, the company's president. The cab walls were shipped to Chicago and assembled on-site. The building's elevator cables were replaced and new controllers were installed, but Advanced Elevator in Aurora, Illinois, was able to salvage the original elevator motors. "It's an investment to get hundred-year-old motors to mesh seamlessly with twenty-first-century technology," said Dahlberg.

Crenshaw Lighting in Floyd, Virginia, manufactured eighteen bronze sconces that illuminate the two entrance vestibules and the elevator lobby. The original fixtures were replaced during the 1950s remodeling. Because none of them could be found, designers had to rely on historical photographs to replicate the lightly antiqued fixtures. Crenshaw's Stefan Morikawa said the pattern for the first one was created by hand and the rest were cast using a lost-wax process to hold intricate details. "We had to create a wax to achieve that 360-degree detailing found in fixtures," he said. The sconces took about four months to make.

"The object was to be as original as possible but use new technology to bring the light levels up to modern standards and provide a means for safety," said lighting consultant Leslie North, principal at Aurora Lighting Design in Grayslake, Illinois. North said she and the architects considered using LED uplighting so that the decorative columns could be seen better, but they ran into cabling issues and did not want to veer far from the original look. "We were trying to get the original aesthetic while getting modern light levels and meeting codes," she said.

Besides the lobby fixtures, Crenshaw manufactured more than two hundred of the building's elevator call lights, as well as custom ceiling fixtures and wall sconces for the upper floors.

The work seemed endless. Vintage doors and transoms were rebuilt, and period patterned glass was created (by UltraGlas in Chatsworth, California) for the upstairs office windows and elevator grilles. Even the office door hardware was refashioned, made to look original but modified with a lever to meet Americans with Disabilities Act requirements.

NEW OFFICE DOOR LOCKS WERE FABRICATED TO MATCH THE ORIGINALS, BUT WERE UPDATED TO MEET MODERN NEEDS.

The work went slowly because it had to be done around the building's tenants. The Monroe never closed a day. A decision was made at the start that tenants would not be forced out. At the time, this seemed to make business sense—rents would offset some of the construction costs—but the decision may have added a year or two to the construction process. It caused the final construction price to skyrocket.

"We replaced all the stairways and elevators in the building, the entire mechanical and electrical systems, with tenants throughout the building during construction," said architect Thomas Lassin. "All of our work had to be phased carefully because of ongoing occupancy. We had to keep the space warm and cool, and we had to always keep corridors and stairways open as emergency exits."

Despite the time and the exacting standards, most everyone involved in the restoration of the Monroe Building came to appreciate and understand what the process meant. "I can't tell you how many tradesmen came up to me and thanked me for the work," said Peder Dahlberg. "They just didn't thank me for getting the job. They thanked me because it gave them a chance to work at the top of their abilities."

**JENNIFER PRITZKER, WHOSE FAMILY DEVELOPED** the Hyatt hotel chain and Marmon Group, will not divulge the cost of restoring the Monroe Building, but she believes that the preservation effort will pay off for her family in the long run.

Besides restoring the building, she had to update it. A mechanical room and a cooling tower were hidden on the roof, a new loading dock was constructed, and the building was reinforced so that it could accommodate the books in the Pritzker Military Museum & Library as well as the new three-story auditorium.

The modern additions—including new bathrooms on each floor—do not look vintage. "These kinds of projects make you walk a fine line," explained Lassin. "You don't want to make up history or give the impression that something is historic or original when it's not. We tried to make good decisions that resulted in a historically accurate rehabilitation. It is a restoration only in the sense that original materials were maintained and repaired to the extent possible."

Said Sean McGowan, chief operating officer of Tawani Enterprises, who oversaw much of the construction: "We see ourselves as preservationists first and developers second." Tawani's goal is to make the Monroe Building self-sustainable and relevant for the twenty-first century, he said.

"We are preserving its ability to service the market on a long-term competitive basis," said Pritzker. "The quality of the building. The management of the project. The method of capitalization. The demand of the market for a functioning iconic building will justify the expense over the long period. This is the definition of a classic."

Ultimately, more than the Monroe Building was saved.

"Yes, we are preserving history," said Lassin. "But we are also preserving the kind of scale and detail that these buildings possess that isn't seen or isn't replicated in new construction. The history of the city is not just the details of the building; it is the history of maintaining districts. This is part of the Historic Michigan Boulevard District and the Michigan Avenue Streetwall. It is part of Chicago."

citibank
citibank

THE FIFTEENTH AND SIXTEENTH FLOOR OF THE MONROE BUILDING FORMS AN ATTIC THAT HAS LONG BEEN A HOME FOR ARTISTS AND ARCHITECTS.

NEW COPPER FLASHING AND THE GREEN-TILE ROOF OF THE MONROE BUILDING ARE HARD TO SEE FROM GRANT PARK OR THE ART INSTITUTE OF CHICAGO.

DORMERS AND SKYLIGHTS BRING EXTRA LIGHT TO THE MONROE BUILDING'S TOP TWO FLOORS.

TERRA-COTTA DETAIL ON THE UNDERSIDE OF THE MONROE BUILDING'S EAVES. AN ORNAMENTAL OWL SITS ATOP THE NEIGHBORING UNIVERSITY CLUB OF CHICAGO.

ABOVE THE FOURTEENTH FLOOR, MANY OF THE MONROE'S VERTICAL PIERS BECOME SPIRALING PILASTERS.

NOBODY ON THE RESTORATION TEAM KNEW THE EXACT COLOR OF THE TERRA COTTA UNTIL THE BUILDING WAS CLEANED.

EACH COURSE OF TERRA COTTA ON THE BUILDING'S FACADE WAS TONED IN ALTERNATE BANDS OF LIGHT AND DARK.

EARLY MORNING LIGHT RAKES THE FACADE OF THE MONROE BUILDING.

THE MICHIGAN AVENUE ENTRANCE VESTIBULE. RESTORATION ARCHITECTS RETURNED SWING DOORS TO THE TWO ENTRANCES.

ARCHITECTURAL FAIENCE IN THE ENTRY VESTIBULE, LOOKING ABOVE THE INNER SET OF DOORS.

CRAZED TILE, SOME ORIGINAL AND SOME NEW, SURROUND AND FILL THE ELEVATOR LOBBY.

1

NEW ELEVATOR LIGHTS AND BRONZE SCONCES.

ORIGINAL ELEVATOR GRILLES WERE CLEANED AND RESTORED. THE ELEVATOR CABS ARE NEW.

HIGH IN THE LOBBY, A MIX OF NORTHWESTERN TERRA COTTA AND ROOKWOOD TILES.

THE BARREL VAULTED CEILING WAS ONCE COVERED IN SMOKE AND GRIME.

LOOKING STRAIGHT UP AT THE ARCHED TILED HALLWAY IN THE LOBBY.

HEADING UPSTAIRS ON THE FIRST-FLOOR STAIRWAY. RIGHT: THE HISTORICALLY ACCURATE FIFTH FLOOR, HEADQUARTERS OF TAWANI ENTERPRISES, WHICH RESTORED THE BUILDING.

THE PRITZKER MILITARY MUSEUM AND LIBRARY OCCUPIES THREE FLOORS OF THE MONROE BUILDING.

NEW
ARRIVALS

THE LIBRARY INTERIOR WAS DESIGNED BY MARC K. ADELMAN OF ATLANTA-BASED TVSDESIGN.

A CENTURY LATER, THE MONROE BUILDING AND UNIVERSITY CLUB STILL FORM AN EASTERN GATEWAY TO CHICAGO'S DOWNTOWN.

# ACKNOWLEDGMENTS

**WRITING AND PRODUCING THIS BOOK** gave us a chance to tell Chicago's architectural history through one building. To understand that building, we relied on Tim Samuelson, Chicago's cultural historian, and Robert Bruegmann, the foremost authority on the architecture of Holabird & Roche. They grasped the significance of the Monroe Building years before anybody else. We also relied on more than a century of scholarship in books, magazines, and newspapers. We hope we add to that work.

Peder Dahlberg, who oversaw the Monroe's restoration, deserves praise for the work he did and for providing all of his resources helping us write about and photograph the building. Architects Thomas Lassin and Michael Voorheis, of Holabird & Root, as well as Dave Linden and Mike Lemmons, of Bulley & Andrews, detailed the years of work that went into the restoration. Also providing key insight were Chris Lee, of Bulley & Andrews Masonry Restoration, and restoration architect Mary Brush.

The book also gave us a chance to rub shoulders and share ideas with true craftsmen, including Jim Robinson, of Rookwood Pottery; Tab Colbert, of Ludwici Roof Tile; Lou Nutini, of Illinois Bronze Works/MTH Industries; Mark and Chris Cronin, of Knickerbocker Roofing & Paving; Janet Zoble, of Promark Management; Al Koenig, of Globe Architectural and Metal; Leslie North, of Aurora Lighting Design; Stefan Morikawa, of Crenshaw Lighting; Jane Skeeter, of UltraGlas, and Sherri Miske, the representative of Gladding, McBean.

Bob Horner, of Winthrop Properties, and architect Patrick FitzGerald shared their plans for the Monroe Building. And Jane Strobeck, of Strobeck Real Estate, detailed the previous ownership of the building and found an early rendering.

Just about everybody who contributed also provided us with valuable plans and restoration photographs, as did the Chicago History Museum. Alexander Vertikoff photographed the building after restoration.

At the Monroe, building engineer Pat Godley took us to the sub-basement and property manager Paul J. Rades let us climb all over the roof. Most important was Sean McGowan, chief operating officer of Tawani Enterprises, and, of course, Jennifer Pritzker, who followed her intuition and has produced a treasure.

Printed in China

ISBN: 978-0-692-25896-5